1st EDITION

Perspectives on Diseases and Disorders

Mood Disorders

Jacqueline Langwith
Book Editor

Detroit • New York • San Francisco • New Haven, Conn • Waterville, Maine • London

Christine Nasso, *Publisher*
Elizabeth Des Chenes, *Managing Editor*

© 2009 Greenhaven Press, a part of Gale, Cengage Learning

For more information, contact:
Greenhaven Press
27500 Drake Rd.
Farmington Hills, MI 48331-3535
Or you can visit our Internet site at gale.cengage.com

For product information and technology assistance, contact us at

Gale Customer Support, 1-800-877-4253
For permission to use material from this text or product, submit all requests online at
www.cengage.com/permissions

Further permissions questions can be emailed to permissionrequest@cengage.com

Articles in Greenhaven Press anthologies are often edited for length to meet page requirements. In addition, original titles of these works are changed to clearly present the main thesis and to explicitly indicate the author's opinion. Every effort is made to ensure that Greenhaven Press accurately reflects the original intent of the authors. Every effort has been made to trace the owners of copyrighted material.

Cover image ©2009 Jupiterimages

LIBRARY OF CONGRESS CATALOGING-IN-PUBLICATION DATA

Mood disorders / Jacqueline Langwith, book editor.
   p. cm. -- (Perspectives on Diseases and Disorders)
Includes bibliographical references and index.
ISBN 978-0-7377-4380-7 (hardcover)
1. Affective disorders. I. Langwith, Jacqueline.
RC537.M6625 2009
616.85'27--dc22

2008055447

Printed in the United States of America
1 2 3 4 5 6 7 13 12 11 10 09

CONTENTS

FOREWORD

"Medicine, to produce health, has to examine disease."
—Plutarch

Independent research on a health issue is often the first step to complement discussions with a physician. But locating accurate, well-organized, understandable medical information can be a challenge. A simple Internet search on terms such as "cancer" or "diabetes," for example, returns an intimidating number of results. Sifting through the results can be daunting, particularly when some of the information is inconsistent or even contradictory. The Greenhaven Press series Perspectives on Diseases and Disorders offers a solution to the often overwhelming nature of researching diseases and disorders.

From the clinical to the personal, titles in the Perspectives on Diseases and Disorders series provide students and other researchers with authoritative, accessible information in unique anthologies that include basic information about the disease or disorder, controversial aspects of diagnosis and treatment, and first-person accounts of those impacted by the disease. The result is a well-rounded combination of primary and secondary sources that, together, provide the reader with a better understanding of the disease or disorder.

Each volume in Perspectives on Diseases and Disorders explores a particular disease or disorder in detail. Material for each volume is carefully selected from a wide range of sources, including encyclopedias, journals, newspapers, nonfiction books, speeches, government documents, pamphlets, organization newsletters, and position papers. Articles in the first chapter provide an authoritative, up-to-date overview that covers symptoms, causes and effects, treatments, cures, and medical advances. The second chapter presents a substantial number of opposing viewpoints on controversial treatments and other current debates relating to the volume topic. The third chapter offers a variety of personal perspectives on the disease or disorder. Patients, doctors, caregivers, and loved ones represent just some of the voices found in this narrative chapter.

Each Perspectives on Diseases and Disorders volume also includes:

- An **annotated table of contents** that provides a brief summary of each article in the volume.
- An **introduction** specific to the volume topic.
- Full-color **charts and graphs** to illustrate key points, concepts, and theories.
- Full-color **photos** that show aspects of the disease or disorder and enhance textual material.
- **"Fast Facts"** that highlight pertinent additional statistics and surprising points.
- A **glossary** providing users with definitions of important terms.
- A **chronology** of important dates relating to the disease or disorder.
- An annotated list of **organizations to contact** for students and other readers seeking additional information.
- A **bibliography** of additional books and periodicals for further research.
- A detailed **subject index** that allows readers to quickly find the information they need.

Whether a student researching a disorder, a patient recently diagnosed with a disease, or an individual who simply wants to learn more about a particular disease or disorder, a reader who turns to Perspectives on Diseases and Disorders will find a wealth of information in each volume that offers not only basic information, but also vigorous debate from multiple perspectives.

INTRODUCTION

"What if the antidepressant Prozac had been available in Van Gogh's time?" This question was frequently asked of psychiatrist and author Peter Kramer in the 1990s while he toured the country talking about his book *Listening to Prozac.* The question's meaning was clear to him. If Vincent van Gogh took Prozac would he have painted *Starry Night*? If Edgar Allan Poe took Prozac would he have written *The Raven*? To many people these are valid questions. Creativity appears to be associated with mental illness, particularly the mood disorders of depression and bipolar disorder. Some people think that treating mood disorders with medication impedes the creative process. However, others believe that medication helps people overcome mood disorders' debilitating symptoms and can help creativity flourish.

Creativity and Mental Illness

Some of the world's most famous creative geniuses are thought to have suffered from mental illness. In her book *Touched with Fire* psychiatrist Kay Redfield Jamison produces a lengthy list of past artists who she believes suffered from bipolar disorder. Based on evidence in their personal and public writings and written accounts by those who knew them, Jamison says Vincent van Gogh and Edgar Allan Poe most likely had bipolar disorder. She also lists twentieth-century writers Ernest Hemingway, Sylvia Plath, and Virginia Woolf, all of whom committed suicide. Others on Jamison's list include writer F. Scott Fitzgerald, poet Lord Byron, and painters Paul Gauguin and Jackson

Pollack. Contemporary artists who have been diagnosed with bipolar disorder include musician Kurt Cobain, the lead singer of Nirvana. Cobain committed suicide in 1994. Musicians Axl Rose and Sinead O'Connor have also been diagnosed with bipolar disorder.

Many famous creative people, such as rocker Kurt Cobain, have had bipolar disorder that led to suicide. (**Kevin Mazur/WireImage/Getty Images**)

Vincent van Gogh is frequently depicted as the epitome of the "tortured artist." Vincent van Gogh was born on March 30, 1853, and he took his life at the age of thirty-seven. His paintings are some of the most valued in the world, fetching tens of millions of dollars. By all accounts Van Gogh was highly emotional and suffered extreme mood swings and long bouts of depression. In one famous event Van Gogh stalked Paul Gauguin—another famous Postimpressionist painter who is thought to have suffered from a mood disorder—with a razor and then cut off the lower part of his own left ear, wrapped it in newspaper, and gave it to a prostitute in the local brothel, saying, "Keep this object carefully." Shortly after this event, Van Gogh committed himself to a mental hospital. A doctor there diagnosed him with epilepsy and "acute mania with hallucinations of sight and hearing." In *Touched with Fire*, Jamison writes, "Van Gogh's symptoms, the natural course of his illness, and his family psychiatric illness—both brothers and one of his sisters suffered psychosis and depression—are completely consistent with a diagnosis of manic-depressive (bipolar disorder) illness."

Is it just coincidence that Van Gogh and other great artists suffered from mental illness, or are mental illness and creativity linked somehow? Scientists have been trying to answer this question. Stanford University professor Terence Ketter says he became interested in the link between creativity and mental illness after noticing that patients who came through the bipolar clinic at Stanford, despite having problems, were bright, motivated people who tended to lead interesting lives. In 2002 Ketter and Connie Strong, another Stanford professor, published the results of a study in which they administered personality, temperament, and creativity tests to groups of healthy individuals, people suffering from a mood disorder, and artists. The results showed that artists were more similar in personality to individuals with manic depression than to healthy people. In 2005 Ketter published the results of another study that showed that children with bipolar disorder scored higher on a creativity index than healthy children. Ketter believes that bipolar patients' creativity stems from their ability to mobilize negative emotion to try to solve their problems. "Discontent is the mother of invention," says Ketter.

The Question of Medication

The apparent link between creativity and depression has caused some people to forgo antidepressant medications or to speak against routinely medicating depressed people. In 2006 Massachusetts Institute of Technology (MIT) student Analucia Berry interviewed several students for an essay about students' attitudes toward depression and Prozac. In her essay "Beavers and Prozac" she describes an MIT student named Catherine who is an artist. Catherine admits to being chronically depressed, but she refuses to take antidepressants for fear of losing her creativity. Catherine says she feels most creative when she is feeling slightly melancholic. In Catherine's view, losing her creativity would greatly outweigh any positive effect she would feel from Prozac. Author and Wake Forest University English professor Eric Wilson also suffers from depression. In his book *Against Happiness* he argues that the world needs sadness and melancholy. In a 2008 interview on National Public Radio, Wilson says he is worried that widespread use of antidepressants might make "sweet sorrow" a thing of the past. According to Wilson, "Melancholy pushes people to think about their relation to the world in new ways and ultimately to relate to the world in a richer, deeper way." About the fact that many great artists have suffered deeply from their depression, Wilson says, perhaps this is "just part of the tragic nature of existence, that sometimes there's a great price to be paid for great works of beauty, for truth. We can look at the lives of Dylan Thomas, Virginia Woolf, Hart

Many creative people feel that depression medications, such as Prozac, have a negative effect on their creativity. (© age fotostock/SuperStock)

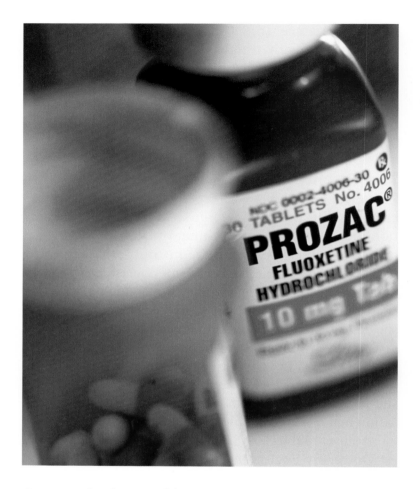

Crane and others and lament the fact that they suffered so. Yet at the same time, we're buoyed, we're overjoyed by the works they left behind." Wilson is worried that medicating depression away could cause human culture to become less creative and less vital.

Other people, however, think that medication can alleviate the pain of a mood disorder without impeding the creative process. They think that if Van Gogh had received treatment for bipolar disorder he might have been even more creative. Peter Kramer, who was asked so often about Van Gogh and Prozac, has written extensively about depression. In his book *Against Depres-*

sion Kramer acknowledges that many people, such as Eric Wilson, think the world would be sterile and dull without depression-inspired artists. However, Kramer disagrees. He believes that depth, complexity, and creativity can flourish without the pain of depression. Says Kramer, "like other diseases, the mental illnesses may lend perspective to art. But the disorders are destructive in dozens of ways. Medications have their problems. But by and large, if my patients do well on medication, they write, paint, compose, and sculpt *better*." Others agree. In *Poets on Prozac* Richard Berlin presents examples of writing from several different poets before, during, and after their treatment for depression, schizophrenia, and other psychiatric disorders. Berlin believes, and the poets' writing examples substantiate, that treating mental illness does not detract from the creative process; it can even enhance it. Gwyneth Lewis, one of the poets profiled in Berlin's book, says: "Depression strips you of everything that makes you feel like a creative, contributing member of a family or society." Antidepressants helped Lewis regain her life and her writing. In 2005 she was named the first national poet of Wales.

In Kramer's, Berlin's, and Lewis's viewpoints, treatments, such as antidepressants, that release sufferers from the painful grips of depression or bipolar disorder can only help the creative process. However, MIT student Catherine and author Eric Wilson think that artists need to feel "blue" in order to tap their creative juices, and they think medication would hamper this process.

Whether treatment helps or hinders the creative process is just one of the many aspects of mood disorders that people are discussing and scientists are studying. In *Perspectives on Diseases and Disorders: Mood Disorders* the contributors discuss the latest research into the causes, symptoms, and treatments of mood disorders; the controversies surrounding them; and the personal stories of people living with mood disorders.

CHAPTER 1

Understanding Mood Disorders

An Overview of Mood Disorders

Robert Scott Dinsmoor and Teresa G. Odle

In the following viewpoint Robert Scott Dinsmoor and Teresa G. Odle provide an overview of mood disorders. According to Dinsmoor and Odle, there are three main classifications of mood disorders: major depression, bipolar disorder, and dysthymia. The symptoms of major depression include a loss of appetite, feelings of worthlessness, fatigue, and disturbed thinking. People suffering from bipolar disorder cycle between a depressed mood and an elevated mood called mania or hypomania. Dysthymia is a milder, more long-lasting form of major depression. The authors say that the most effective treatment for mood disorders is a combination of medication and psychotherapy. Dinsmoor and Odle are nationally published medical writers.

Mood disorders are mental disorders characterized by periods of depression, sometimes alternating with periods of elevated mood.

SOURCE: Robert Scott Dinsmoor and Teresa G. Odle, *The Gale Encyclopedia of Medicine*, Detroit: Gale, 2006. Copyright © 2006 Gale, Cengage Learning. Reproduced by permission of Gale, a part of Cengage Learning.

Photo on facing page. People with mood disorders suffer from severe or prolonged mood states that disrupt their ability to function on a daily basis.
(© Phototake, Inc./Alamy)

Symptoms of depression include loss of appetite, fatigue, difficulties in decision making, and an overwhelming feeling of sadness. (© age fotostock/ SuperStock)

While many people go through sad or elated moods from time to time, people with mood disorders suffer from severe or prolonged mood states that disrupt their daily functioning. Among the general mood disorders classified in the fourth edition (1994) of the *Diagnostic and Statistical Manual of Mental Disorders (DSM-IV)* are major depressive disorder, bipolar disorder, and dysthymia.

Classifying Mood Disorders

In classifying and diagnosing mood disorders, doctors determine if the mood disorder is unipolar or bipolar. When only one extreme in mood (the depressed state) is experienced, this type of depression is called unipolar. Major depression refers to a single severe period of depression, marked by negative or hopeless thoughts and physical symptoms like fatigue. In major depressive disorder, some patients have isolated episodes of depression. In between these episodes, the patient does not feel depressed or have other symptoms associated with depression. Other patients have more frequent episodes.

Bipolar depression or bipolar disorder (sometimes called manic depression) refers to a condition in which people experience two extremes in mood. They alternate between depression (the "low" mood) and mania or hypomania (the "high" mood). These patients go from depression to a frenzied, abnormal elevation in mood. Mania and hypomania are similar, but mania is usually more severe and debilitating to the patient.

Dysthymia is a recurrent or lengthy depression that may last a lifetime. It is similar to major depressive disorder, but dysthymia is chronic, long-lasting, persistent, and mild. Patients may have symptoms that are not as severe as major depression, but the symptoms last for many years. It seems that a mild form of the depression is always present. In some cases, people also may experience a major depressive episode on top of their dysthymia, a condition sometimes referred to as a "double depression."

Causes and Symptoms

Mood disorders tend to run in families. These disorders are associated with imbalances in certain chemicals that carry signals between brain cells (neurotransmitters). These chemicals include serotonin, norepinephrine, and dopamine. Women are more vulnerable to unipolar depression than are men. Major life stressors (like divorce, serious financial problems, death of a family member, etc.) will often provoke the symptoms of depression in susceptible people.

Major depression is more serious than just feeling "sad" or "blue." The symptoms of major depression may include:

- Loss of appetite
- A change in sleep patterns, like not sleeping (insomnia) or sleeping too much
- Feelings of worthlessness, hopelessness, or inappropriate guilt
- Fatigue
- Difficulty in concentrating or making decisions
- Overwhelming and intense feelings of sadness or grief
- Disturbed thinking. The person may also have physical symptoms like stomachaches or headaches.

Bipolar disorder includes mania or hypomania. Mania is an abnormal elevation in mood. The person may be excessively cheerful, have grandiose ideas, and may sleep less. He or she may talk nonstop for hours, have unending enthusiasm, and demonstrate poor judgement. Sometimes the elevation in mood is marked by irritability and hostility rather than cheerfulness. While the person may at first seem normal with an increase in energy, others who know the person well see a marked difference in behavior. The patient may seem to be in a frenzy and often will make poor, bizarre, or dangerous choices in his/her personal and professional lives. Hypomania is not as severe as mania and does not cause the level of impairment in work and social activities that mania can.

Diagnosing and Treating Mood Disorders

Doctors diagnose mood disorders based on the patient's description of the symptoms as well as the patient's family

People with Bipolar Disorder Are Depressed for Almost One-Third of Their Lives

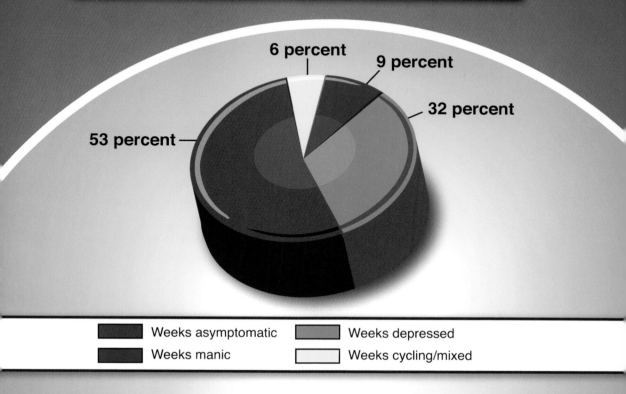

6 percent

9 percent

32 percent

53 percent

Weeks asymptomatic   Weeks depressed

Weeks manic   Weeks cycling/mixed

Taken from: Paul E. Keck Jr. et al., "Bipolar Depression: Best Practices for the Outpatient," *CNS Spectrums*, 2007.

history. The length of time the patient has had symptoms also is important. Generally patients are diagnosed with dysthymia if they feel depressed more days than not for at least two years. The depression is mild but long lasting. In major depressive disorder, the patient is depressed almost all day nearly every day of the week for at least two weeks. The depression is severe. Sometimes laboratory tests are performed to rule out other causes for the symptoms (like thyroid disease). The diagnosis may be confirmed when a patient responds well to medication.

The most effective treatment for mood disorders is a combination of medication and psychotherapy. In fact, a 2003 report revealed that people on medication for bipolar disorder had better results if they also participated in family-focused therapy. The four different classes of drugs used in mood disorders are:

- Heterocyclic antidepressants (HCAs), like amitriptyline (Elavil)
- Selective serotonin reuptake inhibitors (SSRIs), like fluoxetine (Prozac), paroxetine (Paxil), and sertraline (Zoloft)
- Monoamine oxidase inhibitors (MAOIs), like phenelzine sulfate (Nardil) and tranylcypromine sulfate (Parnate)
- Mood stabilizers, like lithium carbonate (Eskalith) and valproate, often used in people with bipolar mood disorders.

A number of psychotherapy approaches are useful as well. Interpersonal psychotherapy helps the patient recognize the interaction between the mood disorder and interpersonal relationships. Cognitive-behavioral therapy explores how the patient's view of the world may be affecting his or her mood and outlook.

When depression fails to respond to treatment or when there is a high risk of suicide, electroconvulsive therapy (ECT) sometimes is used. ECT is believed to affect neurotransmitters like the medications do. Patients are anesthetized and given muscle relaxants to minimize discomfort. Then low-level electric current is passed through the brain to cause a brief convulsion. The most common side effect of ECT is mild, short-term memory loss.

Alternative Treatment

There are many alternative therapies that may help in the treatment of mood disorders, including acupuncture, botanical medicine, homeopathy, aromatherapy, constitutional hydrotherapy, and light therapy. The therapy used is an individual choice. Short-term clinical studies have shown that the herb St. John's wort (*Hypericum perforatum*) can effectively treat some types of depression. Though it appears very safe, the herb may have some side effects and its long-term effectiveness has not been proven. It has not been tested in patients with bipolar disorder. Despite uncertainty concerning its effectiveness, a 2003 report said acceptance of the treatment continues to increase. A poll showed that about 41% of 15,000 science professionals in 62 countries said they would use St. John's wort for mild to moderate depression. Although St. John's wort appears to be a safe alternative to conventional antidepressants, care should be taken, as the herb can interfere with the actions of some pharmaceuticals. The usual dose is 300 mg three times daily. St. John's wort and antidepressant drugs should not be taken simultaneously, so patients should tell their doctor if they are taking St. John's wort. . . .

> **FAST FACT**
>
> An estimated 26.2 percent of Americans aged eighteen and older suffer from a diagnosable mental disorder in a given year, according to the National Institute of Mental Health.

Most cases of mood disorders can be successfully managed if properly diagnosed and treated.

People can take steps to improve mild depression and keep it from becoming worse. They can learn stress management (like relaxation training or breathing exercises), exercise regularly, and avoid drugs or alcohol.

There Are Differences Between Unipolar and Bipolar Depression

Rashmi Nemade, Natalie Staats Reiss, and Mark Dombeck

In the following viewpoint Rashmi Nemade, Natalie Staats Reiss, and Mark Dombeck explain that major depression is called "unipolar depression" because people with the disorder are always on the downside of the "emotional thermometer." On the other hand, people suffering from bipolar disorder cycle between the upside and the downside of the emotional thermometer. Dombeck is the director and Reiss is an editor at MentalHelp.net, an online resource for mental health information and education. Nemade is a contributing writer.

E veryone has days where they feel blah, down, or sad. Typically, these feelings disappear after a day or two, particularly if circumstances change for the better. People experiencing the temporary "blues" don't feel a sense of crushing hopelessness or helplessness, and are able, for the most part, to continue to en-

SOURCE: Rashmi Nemade, Natalie Staats Reiss, and Mark Dombeck, "Introduction to Major Depression (and Other Unipolar Depressions)," MentalHelp.net, September 18, 2007. Reproduced by permission.

gage in regular activities. Prolonged anhedonia (the inability to experience pleasure), hopelessness, and failure to experience an increase in mood in response [to] positive events rarely accompany "normal" sadness. The same may be said for other, more intense sorts of symptoms such as suicidal thoughts and hallucinations (e.g., hearing voices). Instead, such symptoms suggest that serious varieties of depression may be present, including the subject of this document: Major Depressive Disorder (MDD) or (more informally), Major Depression.

Major Depression is a common yet serious medical condition that affects both the mind and body. It is a complex illness, creating physical, psychological, and social symptoms. Although informally, we often use the term "depression" to describe general sadness, the term Major Depression is defined by a formal set of criteria which describe which symptoms must be present before the label may be appropriately used.

FAST FACT

Women are more likely than men to suffer from unipolar depression, while men and women are equally likely to suffer from bipolar depression.

Moods Convey Emotional Temperature

Major Depression is a mood disorder. The term "mood" describes one's emotions or emotional temperature. It is a set of feelings that express a sense of emotional comfort or discomfort. Sometimes, mood is described as a prolonged emotion that colors a person's whole psychic life and state of well-being. For example, if someone is depressed, they may not feel like exercising. By not exercising for long periods of time, they will eventually experience the negative effects of a sedentary lifestyle such as fatigue, muscle aches and pains, and in some cases, heart disease.

Many people are puzzled by the term "Unipolar Depression," which is another term for Major Depression. The term "Unipolar Depression" is used here to differentiate Major Depression from the other famous sort of depression, Bipolar (or Manic) Depression, which is a

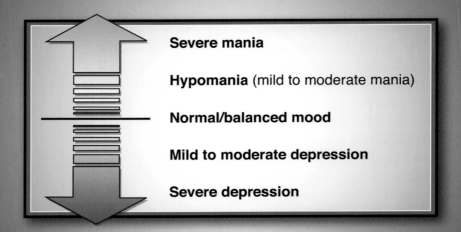

Mood Disorder Spectrum

Severe mania

Hypomania (mild to moderate mania)

Normal/balanced mood

Mild to moderate depression

Severe depression

Taken from: "Symptoms of Bipolar Disorder," HealthyPlace.com.

separate illness. It is helpful to think of mood states as occurring on a continuum. During a particular day or week, people can shift from good (or "up") moods, to bad (or "down") moods, or remain somewhere in the middle ("neutral" mood). A person who experiences significant impairment related to shifting between up and down moods often has Bipolar Disorder. . . . Bipolar Disorder can be envisioned as a seesaw movement back and forth between two poles or mood states ("bi" means "two"). In contrast to people with Bipolar Disorder, people with Major Depression remain on the down mood pole; they do not exhibit mood swings. Because they are stuck on the down or depressed end of the mood continuum, they experience a unipolar ("uni" means "one") mood state.

Depression Causes Widespread Suffering

Mood disorders rank among the top 10 causes of worldwide disability, and Major Depression appears first on the list. Disability and suffering is not limited to the individual diagnosed with MDD. Spouses, children, parents, siblings, and friends of people experiencing Major Depression often experience frustration, guilt, anger, and financial hardship in their attempts to cope with the suffering of their friend or loved one.

Major Depression has a negative impact on the economy as well as the family system. In the workplace, depression is a leading cause of absenteeism and diminished productivity. Although only a minority of people seek professional help to relieve a mood disorder, depressed people are significantly more likely than others to visit a physician. Some people express their sadness in physical ways, and these individuals may undergo extensive and expensive diagnostic procedures and treatments while their mood disorder goes undiagnosed and untreated. As

People with bipolar disorder experience frequent mood swings ranging from elation to severe depression. (© **ClassicStock/Alamy**)

a result, depression-related visits to physicians account for a large portion of health care expenditures.

Although the origins of depression are not yet fully understood, we do know that there are a number of factors that can cause a person to suffer from depression. We also know that people who are depressed cannot simply will themselves to snap out of it. Getting better often requires appropriate treatment. Fortunately, there are a wide array of effective treatments available.

Bipolar Mood Disorders Are Complex Brain Diseases

John McManamy

In the following viewpoint John McManamy discusses bipolar I and bipolar II, the two main types of bipolar disorders classified in the *Diagnostic and Statistical Manual of Mental Disorders, 4th Edition (DSM-IV)*. Bipolar I, which McManamy calls "raging bipolar," and bipolar II, which he refers to as "swinging bipolar," are characterized by varying degrees of mania, psychosis, and depression. According to McManamy, bipolar disorders are challenging to diagnose and treat. McManamy is an author and the founder of McMan's Depression and Bipolar Web, an online mental health resource.

L et's start with the boring stuff:

The *DSM-IV* [*Diagnostic and Statistical Manual of Mental Disorders, 4th Edition*] (the diagnostic Bible published by the American Psychiatric Association) divides bipolar disorder into two types, rather unimaginatively labeled bipolar I and bipolar II. "Raging" and "Swinging" are far more apt.

SOURCE: John McManamy, "Bipolar Disorder—A Closer Look," McMan's Depression and Bipolar Web, February 10, 2008. Reproduced by permission.

Negative moods and behaviors due to bipolar disorders include depression, anxiety, irritability, and physical violence. (© redsnapper/Alamy)

Raging Bipolar

Raging bipolar (I) is characterized by at least one full-blown manic episode lasting at least one week or any duration if hospitalization is required. This may include inflated self-esteem or grandiosity, decreased need for sleep, being more talkative than usual, flight of ideas, distractibility, increase in goal-oriented activity, and excessive involvement in risky activities.

The symptoms are severe enough to disrupt the patient's ability to work and socialize, and may require hospitalization to prevent harm to himself or others. The patient may lose touch with reality to the point of being psychotic.

The other option for raging bipolar is at least one "mixed" episode on the part of the patient. The *DSM-IV* is uncharacteristically vague as to what constitutes mixed, an accurate reflection of the confusion within the psychiatric profession. More tellingly, a mixed episode is almost impossible to explain to the public. One is literally "up" and "down" at the same time.

The pioneering German psychiatrist Emil Kraepelin around the turn of the twentieth century divided mania into four classes, including hypomania, acute mania, delusional or psychotic mania, and depressive or anxious mania (ie mixed). . . . Different manias often demand different medications. Lithium, for example, is effective for classic mania while Depakote is the treatment of choice for mixed mania.

The next *DSM* is likely to expand on mania. In a grand rounds lecture delivered at UCLA [University of California at Los Angeles] in March 2003, Susan McElroy MD of the University of Cincinnati outlined her four "domains" of mania, namely:

> As well as the "classic" *DSM-IV* symptoms (eg euphoria and grandiosity), there are also "psychotic" symptoms, with "all the psychotic symptoms in schizophrenia also in mania." Then there is "negative mood and behavior," including depression, anxiety, irritability, violence, or suicide. Finally, there are "cognitive symptoms," such as racing thoughts, distractibility, disorganization, and inattentiveness. Unfortunately, "if you have thought disorder problems, you get all sorts of points for schizophrenia, but not for mania unless there are racing thoughts and distractibility."

Kay Jamison in *Touched with Fire* writes: "The illness encompasses the extremes of human experience. Thinking can range from florid psychosis, or 'madness,' to patterns of unusually clear, fast, and creative associations, to retardation so profound that no meaningful activity can occur."

The *DSM-IV* has given delusional or psychotic mania its own separate diagnosis as schizoaffective disorder—a sort of hybrid between bipolar disorder and schizophrenia, but this may be a completely artificial distinction. These days, psychiatrists are acknowledging psychotic features as part of the illness, and are finding the newer generation of antipsychotics such as Zyprexa effective in treating mania. As Terence Ketter MD of Stanford told the 2001 National Depressive and Manic Depressive Association Conference, it may be inappropriate to have a discrete cut between the two disorders when both may represent part of a spectrum. . . .

Depression is not a necessary component of raging bipolar, though it is strongly implied what goes up must come down. The *DSM-IV* subdivides bipolar I into those presenting with a single manic episode with no past major depression, and those who have had a past major depression (corresponding to the *DSM-IV* for unipolar depression).

FAST FACT

Bipolar disorder affects 5.7 million American adults, approximately 2.6 percent of the adult population per year, according to the *National Alliance Mental Illness Fact Sheet*.

Swinging Bipolar

Swinging bipolar (II) presumes at least one major depressive episode, plus at least one hypomanic episode over at least four days. The same characteristics as mania are evident, with the disturbance of mood observable by others, but the episode is not enough to disrupt normal functioning or necessitate hospitalization, and there are no psychotic features.

Those in a state of hypomania are typically the life of the party, the salesperson of the month, and more often than not the best-selling author or Fortune 500 mover and shaker, which is why so many refuse to seek treatment. But the same condition can also turn on its victim, resulting in bad decision-making, social embarrassments, wrecked relationships, and projects left unfinished.

Hypomania can also occur in those with raging bipolar, and may be the prelude to a full-blown manic episode.

While working on the American Psychiatric Association's latest *DSM* version of bipolar (*IV-TR*), Trisha Suppes MD, PhD of the University of Texas Medical Center in Dallas carefully read its criteria for hypomania, and had an epiphany. "I said, wait," she told a UCLA grand rounds lecture in April 2003 and webcast the same day, "where are all those patients of mine who are hypomanic and say they don't feel good?"

Apparently, there is more to hypomania than mere mania lite. Dr Suppes had in mind a different type of patient, say one who experiences road rage and can't sleep. Why was there no mention of that in hypomania? she wondered. A subsequent literature search yielded virtually no data.

The *DSM* alludes to mixed states where full-blown mania and major depression collide in a raging sound and fury, but nowhere does it account for more subtle manifestations, often the type of states many bipolar patients may spend a good deal of their lives in. . . .

Clinicians commonly refer to these under-the-*DSM* radar mixed states as dysphoric [distressed] hypomania or agitated depression, often using the terms interchangeably. Dr Suppes defines the former as "an energized depression," which she and her colleagues made the object of a prospective study of 919 outpatients from the Stanley Bipolar Treatment Network. Of 17,648 patient visits, 6,993 involved depressive symptoms, 1,294 hypomania, and 9,361 were euthymic (symptom-free).

Of the hypomania visits, 60 percent (783) met her criteria for dysphoric hypomania. Females accounted for 58.3 percent of those with the condition. . . .

Bipolar Depression, the Downward Aspect

Major depression is part of the *DSM-IV* criteria for swinging bipolar, but the next edition of the *DSM* may have to revisit what constitutes the downward aspect of this illness. At present, the *DSM-IV* criteria for major unipolar depression pinch-hits for a genuine bipolar depression diagnosis. On the surface, there is little to distinguish between bipolar and unipolar depression, but certain "atypical" features may indicate different forces at work inside the brain.

According to Francis Mondimore MD, assistant professor at Johns Hopkins and author of "Bipolar Disorder: A Guide for Patients and Families," talking to a 2002 DRADA [Depression and Related Affective Disorders Association] conference, people with bipolar depression are more likely to have psychotic features and slowed-down depressions (such as sleeping too much) while those with unipolar depression are more prone to crying spells and significant anxiety (with difficulty falling asleep).

Because bipolar II patients spend far more time depressed than hypomanic (50 percent depressed vs one percent hypomanic, according to a 2002 NIMH [National Institute of Mental Health] study) misdiagnosis is common. . . . The implications for treatment are enormous. All too often, bipolar II patients are given just an antidepressant for their depression, which may confer no clinical benefit, but which can drastically worsen the outcome of their illness, including switches into mania or hypomania and cycle acceleration. Bipolar depression calls for a far more sophisticated meds approach, which makes it absolutely essential that those with bipolar II get the right diagnosis.

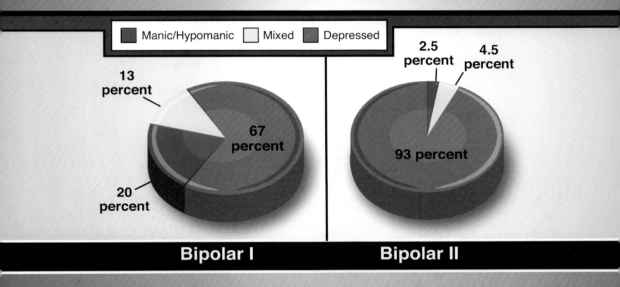

People with Bipolar II Disorder Are Depressed More Often

Bipolar I and II: Frequency of Depressive Symptoms

■ Manic/Hypomanic □ Mixed ■ Depressed

Bipolar I

13 percent

67 percent

20 percent

Bipolar II

2.5 percent

4.5 percent

93 percent

Taken from: Paul E. Keck Jr. et al., "Bipolar Depression: Best Practices for the Outpatient," *CNS Spectrums*, 2007.

This bears emphasis: The hypomanias of bipolar II—at least the ones with no mixed features—are generally easily managed or may not present a problem. But until those hypomanias are identified, a correct diagnosis may not be possible. And without that diagnosis, your depression—the real problem—will not get the right treatment, which could prolong your suffering for years.

Distinguishing Bipolar I from Bipolar II

Dividing bipolar into I and II arguably has more to do with diagnostic convenience than true biology. A University of Chicago/Johns Hopkins study, however, makes a strong case for a genetic distinction. That study found a greater sharing of alleles (one of two or more alternate forms of a gene) along the chromosome 18q21 in siblings with bipolar II than mere randomness would account for.

A 2003 NIMH study tracking 135 bipolar I and 71 bipolar II patients for up to 20 years found:

- Both BP I and BP II patients had similar demographics and ages of onset at first episode.
- Both had more lifetime co-occurring substance abuse than the general population.
- BP II had "significantly higher lifetime prevalence" of anxiety disorders, especially social and other phobias.
- BP Is had more severe episodes at intake.
- BP IIs had "a substantially more chronic course, with significantly more major and minor depressive episodes and shorter inter-episode well intervals."

Nevertheless, for many people, bipolar II may be bipolar I waiting to happen.

A likely candidate for the *DSM-V [DSM, 5th Edition]* as bipolar III is "cyclothymia," listed in the *DSM* as a separate disorder, characterized by symptoms (but not necessarily full episodes of) hypomania and mild depression. One third of those with cyclothymia are eventually diagnosed with bipolar, lending credence to the "kindling" theory of bipolar disorder, that if left untreated in its early stages the illness will break out into something far more severe later on. . . .

A Bipolar Pill?

So little is actually known about the illness that the pharmaceutical industry has yet to develop a drug to treat its symptoms. Lithium, the best-known mood stabilizer, is a common salt, not a proprietary drug. Drugs used as mood stabilizers—Depakote, Neurontin, Lamictal, Topamax, and Tegretol—came on the market as antiseizure medications for treating epilepsy. Antidepressants were developed with unipolar depression in mind, and antipsychotics went into production to treat schizophrenia.

Inevitably, a "bipolar" pill will find its way to the market, and there will be an eager queue of desperate people lining up to be treated. Make no mistake, there is nothing glamorous or romantic about an illness that destroys up to one in five of those who have it, and wreaks havoc on the survivors, not to mention their families. The streets and prisons are littered with wrecked lives. Vincent van Gogh may have created great works of art, but his death in his brother's arms at age 37 was not a pretty picture.

The standard propaganda about bipolar is that it is the result of a chemical imbalance in the brain, a physical condition not unlike diabetes. For the purposes of gaining acceptance in society, most people with bipolar seem to go along with this blatant half-truth.

True, a chemical storm is raging in the brain, but the analogy to the one taking place in the diabetic's pancreas is totally misleading. Unlike diabetes and other physical diseases, bipolar defines who we are, from the way we perceive colors and listen to music to how we taste our food. We don't HAVE bipolar. We ARE bipolar, for both better and worse.

A Blessing and a Challenge

In one way, it's akin to being God's chosen people. As God's chosen, we are prime candidates for God's wrath, but even as God strikes the final blow—as the old Jewish saying goes—he provides the eventual healing. In a way that only God can understand, God has bestowed on us a great blessing. Living with this blessing is both a challenge and a terrible burden, but in the end we hope to emerge from this ordeal as better people, more compassionate toward our fellow beings and just a little bit closer to God.

Children with Bipolar Disorder and Their Families Face Many Challenges

Mary Carmichael

In the following viewpoint Mary Carmichael tells the story of ten-year-old Max Blake, who was diagnosed with bipolar disorder when he was two years old. According to Carmichael, many doctors are skeptical that toddlers can have bipolar disorder. However, Max's doctors and other psychiatrists are convinced that the debilitating disorder afflicts many young children. Carmichael's story reveals a family—Max and his parents, Amy and Richie Blake—struggling to lead normal lives with normal hopes and dreams. But Max is far from normal. He has been on at least thirty-eight different psychoactive drugs in his ten years of life, he suffers from extreme mood swings, and he cannot do many of the things that average kids do. Despite the difficulties, Max has hopes like any other kid—he wants to go to college and become an animator. His parents can only hope his wish comes true. Carmichael is an author and writes about health and science issues for *Newsweek* and *The Boston Globe Sunday Magazine*.

This is the story of a family: a mother, a father and a son. It is, in many ways, a horror story. Terrible things happen. People scream and cry and hurt each other; they say and do things that they later wish they hadn't. The source of their pain is bipolar disorder, a mental illness that results in recurring bouts of mania and depression. It is an elusive disease that no parent fully understands, that some doctors do not believe exists in children, that almost everyone stigmatizes. But this is also a love story. Good things happen. A couple sticks together, a child tries to do better, teachers and doctors and friends help out. Max Blake and his parents may not have much in common with other families. They are a family nonetheless. That is what has mattered most to Amy and Richie Blake since Oct. 31, 1997, the day their son took his first ragged breath.

Born Screaming

Max came into the world with a hole in his heart. Struggling to be born, he lost oxygen, and doctors performed an emergency C-section. Recovering from the operation, Amy feared her infant son would need surgery, too, but the doctors said the hole would close with time. Four days later the Blakes wrapped their baby in a blanket and brought him home to their little house in Peabody, Mass. Richie, a former Marine, was working as a county corrections officer. Amy was a promising divorce lawyer at a firm in nearby Boston. . . .

The mothers of bipolar kids often say their babies are born screaming. These are children who live at the extremes: so giddy they can't speak in sentences, so low they refuse to speak at all. Unlike bipolar adults, they flit rapidly between emotions; sometimes they seem to feel everything at once. At least 800,000 children in the United States have been diagnosed as bipolar, no doubt some of them wrongly. The disease is hard to pin down. The bipolar brain is miswired, but no one knows why

Many parents of babies with bipolar disorder say their babies are born screaming. (© Garry Gay/Alamy)

it develops that way. There are many drugs, but it's unclear how they work. Often, they don't work at all, and they may interfere with normal brain growth. There are no studies on their long-term effects in children. Yet untreated bipolar disorder can be disastrous; 10 percent of sufferers commit suicide. Parents must choose between two wrenching options: treat their children and risk a bad outcome, or don't treat and risk a worse one. No matter what they do, they are in for uncertainty and pain.

Amy knew none of this when Max was born. She did know new motherhood was tough. Max never slept through the night, and neither did she. He cried for hours at a time. He banged his head against his crib and screamed until his face burned red. Nursing, cuddling, pacifiers—none of them helped. At 2 A.M., at 3, at 4 and 5 and 6, Amy cradled her son, trying to believe this was typical infant irritability, the kind her friends with kids had warned her about. It must be colic or gas, she thought, as Max howled another day into being. Exhausted, mystified, she made jokes—he was born on Halloween, she ate too many spicy chicken wings before delivery—trying to explain how a baby too young to hold up his head could raise such hell.

Not Like the Babies in the Parenting Books

After a year, the jokes gave way to worry. Max was reaching and surpassing his milestones, walking by 10 months and talking in sentences by age 1, but he wasn't like the babies in parenting books. Richie carried his son to the backyard and tried to put him down, but Max shrank back in his father's arms; he hated the feel of the grass beneath his small bare feet. Amy gave Max a bath and turned on the exhaust fan; he put his hands over his ears and screamed. At 13 months, he lined up dozens of Hot Wheels in the same direction, and when Amy nudged one out of order, he shrieked "like you'd just cut his arm off." At day care, he terrorized his teachers and playmates. He wasn't the biggest kid in the class, but he attacked without provocation or warning, biting hard enough to leave teeth marks. Every day, he hit and kicked and spat. Worries became guilt. Amy had been overweight and dehydrated in pregnancy. Was Max so explosive because she had done something wrong?

By 18 months, the day-care facility was threatening to throw Max out, and the Blakes were desperate. Richie, the drill sergeant, tried the strict discipline he'd grown up with—he said no, he withheld TV and dessert, he spanked. It didn't work. Amy, the lawyer, tried bargaining with her toddler. That didn't work either. Amy and Richie started to fight about how to raise their son. The family's pediatrician had been treating kids for decades—he had once been Amy's doctor—but he had no answers. All he could say was that this wasn't the terrible twos come early. It was bigger than anything he could fix, and if the Blakes wanted help, they would have to look for it 20 miles down the road.

The Blakes started calling doctors in Boston. After three months of trying, they got through to Joseph Jankowski, chief of child psychiatry at Tufts–New England Medical Center, and scheduled an appointment for Nov. 18, just after Max's 2nd birthday. Jankowski ran several lab tests, but they showed little except for slightly high levels of a metabolic enzyme. He ordered a brain scan and sat down with his interns to watch his new patient. Max behaved as usual: he screamed and bit Amy, then gathered up pieces of paper to draw on, only to rip them to shreds. After an hour, Jankowski said he thought Max might have bipolar disorder. He told the Blakes little else.

Diagnosis: Bipolar Disorder

To the Blakes, bipolar disorder was as foreign as dengue fever. Amy had heard of "manic-depression," but that was a serious illness, one that didn't strike children. Although the National Institute of Mental Health (NIMH) estimates that 5.7 million American adults are affected by the disorder, most doctors, then as now, consider it impossible to diagnose in toddlers. There are still those who joke that every child is "bipolar": up, down, at the mercy of emotion. Amy had her doubts as well. She sat in Jankowski's office and wondered if she should get a second opinion. Worn down, she looked at the degrees on his wall, at the name embroidered on his white coat. "Well," she thought, "I hope he knows what he's talking about."

Jankowski wanted to put Max on a low dose of De-pakote, a drug used for seizures, migraines and bipolar disorder. Amy was used to migraine medications—she'd had the headaches for years—and she and some of her family members had taken antidepressants. Richie was more wary. Like many people, he didn't think children should be on powerful psychoactive meds. He worried about side effects, a concern that would dog him and Amy for years to come. Max lasted on Depakote for just three weeks. He wasn't eating and couldn't sleep. Jankowski tried Zyprexa, an antipsychotic. Within days, Max started eating again. For the first time Amy could remember, he slept like the baby he was. "Good," Amy thought. "We'll keep him on this for a few weeks, like an antibiotic. Then he'll get well and we'll move on."

On Feb. 4, Jankowski said he had a diagnosis. Amy was hoping for something with a cure—"something like a brain tumor, even, something we could read about and understand and fix." Most likely, she thought, it would be attention-deficit/hyperactivity disorder [ADHD]; her friends' kids all had that. Richie thought that whatever Max had, he might grow out of it, the way the hole in his heart had healed on its own. But Jankowski had little com-fort for the Blakes. Their son's problem was serious and incurable: a life sentence. Jankowski's first impression had been borne out. Max was bipolar. Amy and Richie took their son home, and Amy started writing in a notebook that would become a complete log of Max's medical his-tory: "dx [diagnosis]: Bipolar Disorder, Hyperactivity." Then she closed the notebook. Max was screaming again. There was one good thing about this strange diagnosis, she thought: at least it meant she wasn't a bad mother.

Bipolar Diagnoses Not Common for Children

At the time, pediatric bipolar disorder was obscure, even within child psychiatry. Doctors at Massachusetts General Hospital (MGH) fully described the disorder just four years before Max's diagnosis. In 1995, child psychiatrist Joseph Biederman and his protégée Janet Wozniak reported that 16 percent of the kids in their clinic had a form of the illness. "Back then it was considered so rare in children that you might see one in your entire career," says Wozniak. "But we'd been blind to children who were right in front of us." Doctors had missed the fact that their young patients were bouncing between pathological highs and lows, she says: if they saw kids on the upswing, they diagnosed hyperactivity, and if they saw the down side, they diagnosed depression. The MGH team's ideas left many doctors skeptical, but other psychiatrists followed them closely.

Scientists now know that bipolar children have too much activity in a part of the brain called the amygdala, which regulates emotions, and not enough in the prefrontal cortex, the seat of rational thought. "They get so emotional that they can't think," says Mani Pavuluri, a child psychiatrist at the University of Illinois at Chicago. More than the rest of us, a bipolar child perceives the world as a dramatic and dangerous place. If he is shown a picture of a neutral face, he may see it as angry. Show him one that really is angry, and his prefrontal cortex will shut down while his amygdala lights up like a firecracker. The typical result: a fury that feeds on itself. Neurological research has its limits, though, and bipolar disorder still cannot be identified based on brain scans. Diagnosing it is more art than science. Many psychiatrists think that in the years since Max's diagnosis, doctors have erred on the side of seeing it everywhere, mislabeling kids and creating a lucrative market for drug companies. Even one of Max's docs says he thinks nine out of 10 kids with the bipolar label have been wrongly classified. But this sort of debate doesn't much interest Amy. "I don't care what diagnosis Max has," she says. "To me, the concern is, what are we going to do about it?"

So Many Meds, but Not Any Better

In the months after his diagnosis, Max's med log filled up with drug after drug, but he didn't get any better. His private day care kicked him out at 28 months, and the Blakes transferred him to their best remaining option, a public-school special-education program. Now he was surrounded by children with physical or serious learning disabilities, in the care of people who were neither trained nor able to handle such a small, angry bull. Amy would drop him off in the morning, only to arrive at her Boston office and find a message from a teacher telling her to drive back to Peabody and pick him up. There were whole months when he was suspended and the Blakes were stuck at home. Something had to change.

Amy had never stopped thinking about a second opinion. Through a friend, she heard of Jean Frazier, a child psychiatrist at McLean Hospital in Belmont, Mass., who was interested in behavioral therapies as well as drugs. On Dec. 19, 2000—a year, a month and a day after Max's first visit with Jankowski—the Blakes took their 3-year-old to Frazier's office. Max started off in good spirits, but as the appointment wore on, he began to fidget. He refused to look at Frazier when she asked him questions. He tried to bite Richie. He told Amy he wanted to go home. Instead, the Blakes stayed, and Frazier started asking questions again, this time in a whisper. Now Max paid attention, and Frazier realized something: he had been irritated by the sound of her voice. Max couldn't tolerate normal volumes of speech. In her notes, she wrote that he was "a handsome

> **FAST FACT**
>
> In every generation since World War II, there is a higher incidence and an earlier age of onset of bipolar disorder and depression, according to the Child and Adolescent Bipolar Disorder Foundation.

young man with dark hair and a twinkle in his eye." She agreed that he had classic symptoms of bipolar disorder, but she ordered a fresh round of brain scans and blood tests. She told the Blakes she wanted to streamline some of Max's meds. They asked about play therapy, which Jankowski had discouraged. She gave them a referral. More important, she gave them hope.

Max was still adrift in the public schools' special-ed program, and soon he would need to go to kindergarten. Under state and federal disability laws, the district had to pay for him to attend private school if it couldn't meet his needs. Hoping to keep Max in the public-school system, Peabody administrators designed a special curriculum for him. He lasted six weeks, punching and cursing and vandalizing the walls, before they gave up and agreed to send him to the Manville School, part of the Judge Baker Children's Center in Boston, at a cost of $64,000 a year. Manville looked like a regular school, with desks and chairs and a brightly colored mural in the lobby, but it was staffed by social workers and psychologists. It had three teachers for every eight students and almost as many time-out rooms as classrooms. Amy bought a huge three-ring binder where she kept every teacher's note about her son's school-day behavior, the way another mother might save book reports and drawings of dinosaurs. She also found a babysitter, Jenny Mellor, who could watch Max in the afternoons. Richie arranged to spend more time at home, too. He became a firefighter; he had to sleep at the firehouse two nights a week, but that meant he could spend the following days with his son.

Life Still Tumultuous

For all the support he was getting, Max's life was still a series of upheavals. In the space of one year, he tried eight psychoactive medications. Despite all the meds—and in part, because of them—he was an emotional wreck. Amy learned to recognize a look in his eyes. When she saw it, she'd think, "Here comes the devil." In January 2002, 4-year-old Max said he wanted to "freeze to death." In June, he ran away; Amy found him hiding under a neighbor's car. Max seemed to think his imaginary friends were real. His parents wondered if he was hearing voices. In the grocery store, he heard a woman laughing in the next aisle and broke down—he thought she was laughing at him.

By now, Amy and Richie were feeling stranded. Max couldn't go to birthday parties, so Amy quietly tossed the invitations in the trash. Some of the Blakes' friends stopped calling. Amy's mother started e-mailing her "cures" for bipolar disorder she'd found on the Web. Amy wondered if Max's own relatives thought he was "damaged goods." Strangers were no more understanding. One afternoon at the mall, Max threw a fit, and a woman walked up to Amy and told her people like her shouldn't be allowed to have children.

Even at home, Amy and Richie weren't safe from judgment. At their most strained, they turned on each other. Richie had been a patient person before Max came along, but now his patience was worn "as thin as a sheet of paper." Bipolar disorder runs strongly in families, so in the heat of their arguments, Amy and Richie both yelled the worst thing they could think of: "He's your kid! It's your fault!" . . .

Bipolar Disorder Often Gets Worse with Age

By 7 ½, Max was on so many different drugs that Frazier and his parents could no longer tell if they were helping or hurting him. He was suffering from tics, blinking his eyes, clearing his throat and "pulling his clothes like he wanted to get out of his skin," says Richie. In February 2005, under Frazier's supervision, the Blakes took Max off all his meds. With the chemicals out of his system, Max was not the same child he had been at 2. He was worse. Bipolar disorder often gets more serious with age. The brain also reacts to some drugs by remodeling itself, and its dopamine receptors end up naked and sensitive. When the drugs are removed, it's a shock. Off his meds, Max became delusional and paranoid. He imagined Amy was poisoning him and refused to eat anything she cooked. He talked about death constantly and slept little more than two hours a night. Within a month Frazier had put him back on medication, but with a caveat: she wanted to place him in a short-term bed in a child psych ward.

This move did not sit well with the Blakes. They visited Max every day in the hospital but were disturbed to find that many parents with kids on the ward didn't do likewise. They also worried that Max wasn't getting proper treatment. Doctors couldn't check his med levels because he wouldn't sit still for blood tests. Finally, after three weeks, Amy and Richie held him down, and the resulting test showed his levels of lithium were indeed too low to do any good. Against Frazier's advice, they pulled Max out of the hospital and vowed never to send him away again. Two months later he jumped out his bedroom window.

Making Peace with Medication

Today, Max's med log is jammed full of papers: prescription sheets, printouts from Web sites, business cards from doctors. At 10, he has been on 38 different psychoactive drugs. The meds have serious side effects. They have made Max gain weight, and because he's still growing, they frequently need to be changed. The Blakes are aware that many people think their child—any child—should not be on so many drugs. They aren't always happy about it either. But to some degree, they have made their peace with medication.

Max's prognosis has also grown more complex in the seven and a half years since Jankowski first labeled him as bipolar and hyperactive. "He's oppositional-defiant, he's dyslexic, he's ADHD, he's OCD [has obsessive-compulsive disorder]," says Amy. "Give me an initial and he has it." Bipolar children, especially those diagnosed

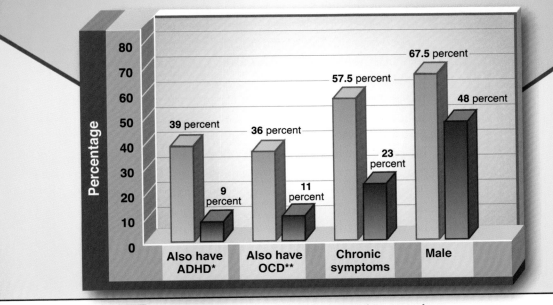

Children with Bipolar Disorder May Also Have Other Disorders

Those diagnosed with bipolar disorder before age twelve are more likely to be male, to have other disorders, and to have chronic, or ongoing, symptoms.

Diagnosed with bipolar disorder before twelve years of age

Diagnosed with bipolar disorder after twelve years of age

*Attention deficit hyperactivity disorder   **Obsessive–compulsive disorder

Taken from: Patrice Wendling, "Irritability, Aggression Rule in Early Bipolar," *Clinical Psychiatry News,* 35.7, July 2007, p. 22 (1).

early, often have such a litany of disorders. The bipolar brain tries to compensate for its weak prefrontal cortex by roping in other areas to help; these areas may now become dysfunctional, too. Child psychiatrists thus face an enormous practical challenge: they often can't treat one disorder without affecting another one. "It's like a balloon where you push on one side and the other side pops out," says Wozniak, the MGH psychiatrist who helped define childhood bipolar disorder. With kids like Max, she adds, parents often have to settle for "just having one part of the symptoms reduced."

Max's life has improved in some ways since his early childhood. Manville has given him a social life. He still has violent tantrums at school, but he also has a best friend, a sweet blond boy with a mild anxiety disorder. Last year he won a "Welcome Wagon" award after teachers noticed he was always the first to show new students around. When his classmates have outbursts of their own, he talks them down. "He'll say that maybe they need to take some space, take a deep breath, leave the classroom," says his teacher, Julie Higgins. He has not, however, figured out how to talk himself down, and for all he has progressed as a classmate, he struggles as a student. Technically, Max is in fourth grade—Manville does not separate grade levels—but he is behind in some subjects. He loves science and art, but he has a hard time reading, and although he is creative, he can't put his ideas in a coherent order. Even holding a pencil for more than a few minutes can be a challenge. "Sometimes you can look at him and you know his disorder has captured him," says the school's director, Jim Prince. "But we can't abandon him. We have to be able to hold on to him, sometimes literally, but also emotionally, to help him come out on the other side." . . .

What Is the Future for Children Like Max?

Max will never truly be OK. In a few years, he will hit puberty, and at that point things will get even more complicated. Teenage rebellion is one thing; a bipolar teenager's rebellion can end in tragedy. "What happens the first time he says to me, 'I'm not taking my pills'?" says Amy. "I can't put them down his throat." She also worries about the end of 10th grade, which is as far as the Manville School goes. Amy doesn't think Max will go back to public school in Peabody, which means he'll have to find another special school or he'll never go to college. Max hasn't processed that yet; he wants to be an animator and has already set his sights on the Massachusetts College of Art and Design. Amy hasn't really processed it either. Every year she puts money in a college account, although she knows the money almost certainly won't be used for tuition. "I want to believe that Max will have this great normal life, but I don't know what's going to happen," she says. "I wouldn't be able to get up in the morning if I thought about it. So I don't anymore."

There are scientists who have thought about the future of children like Max in great depth. Many still think bipolar disorder is vastly overdiagnosed, but they agree that those who have it face a long, rough road. Two years ago the NIMH released findings from a large study of kids diagnosed between 7 and 17. The ones who fared badly had an early onset of the disorder, as well as psychosis, anxiety, ADHD and a tendency to switch quickly between mania and depression. Max has all these. His chances do not look good.

For now, though, his 18th birthday is a long way off. The Blakes are focusing on making it to his 11th. They have found things to look forward to. "We have Max for better or worse, and there's a lot of worse, but there's a lot of better, too," Amy says. "I'm really lucky because I have a kid who can hug me and tell me he loves me, and there are a lot of autistic kids at Manville whose parents never get that. Through all the tears and the hitting and the 'I hate you,' I get to hear 'I love you'."

There was a night last month when Max was calm, and after he finished his homework, he curled up in an easy chair with Amy. She was reading him a book, and although it was only 7:45 his eyelids were fluttering. Eventually he began to whine, and Amy asked him if he was about to start a fight. "Probably," he said. "Let's just get it over with." But he didn't fight. Instead, he was quiet for a few minutes, then he looked at her and said, "Your heart is the size of the world." What he may not realize now, although he surely will someday, is that it has to be.

Brain Imaging Techniques May Lead to Better Treatments for Mood Disorders

National Institute of Mental Health

In the following article the National Institute of Mental Health (NIMH) discusses brain imaging research showing that the brains of people suffering with mood disorders function differently than the brains of healthy people. Using positron emission tomography (PET) and functional magnetic resonance imaging (fMRI) techniques, scientists found that people suffering from depression have abnormal brain reactions that prevent them from experiencing pleasure. Scientists found that when compared to healthy brains, depressed brains released smaller amounts of the neurotransmitter dopamine and had less activity in the cerebral cortex during pleasurable experiences. Scientists also found that the brains of children with bipolar disorder function abnormally when the children are frustrated. The NIMH hopes that imaging children's brains during frustrating experiences may enable doctors to distinguish ADHD (attention deficit/hyperactivity disorder) from bipolar disorder and ensure that kids are properly diagnosed and treated. The National Institute of Mental Health is a U.S. agency dedicated to research focused on the understanding, treatment, and prevention of mental disorders and the promotion of mental health.

SOURCE: "Imaging Identifies Brain Regions and Chemicals Underlying Mood Disorders; May Lead to Better Treatments," National Institute of Mental Health, May 6, 2008. www.nimh.gov.

Recently developed imaging techniques allow the mapping of the brain circuits and chemical systems believed responsible for a range of mood abnormalities including depression and bipolar disorder, and hold promise for improved treatments, scientists say.

They spoke today [May 6, 2008] at a press conference involving presenters from symposia sponsored by the National Institute of Mental Health (NIMH), a part of the National Institutes of Health, during the American Psychiatric Association Annual Meeting. . . .

"These studies contribute new information about how the brain malfunctions in depression and bipolar disorder, what goes wrong with brain chemicals, and where in the brain the problems arise," says Ellen Leibenluft, MD, of NIMH. "We find that the brain systems involved and the exact nature of the difficulties, differs among patients, even when those patients have similar symptoms. Eventually, data like these will allow us to develop more individualized and targeted treatments for these illnesses."

Fewer Serotonin Receptors

Major depressive disorder (MDD) is an illness with high prevalence in the population, yet its underlying biological mechanisms are complex, with genetic and environmental factors influencing each other and leading to varying levels of vulnerability and resiliency.

New studies of two brain chemical systems thought to be involved in the modulation and response to stressful events finds that both are altered in untreated patients with MDD. "Dysregulation of these systems is present in patients diagnosed with MDD and we are studying their relationship with specific characteristics of the illness, such as severity and treatment response," says Jon-Kar Zubieta, MD, PhD, of the University of Michigan.

Using molecular imaging with positron emission tomography [PET], Zubieta and his colleagues traced levels of the receptors for the brain chemicals serotonin and

Researchers are using magnetic resonance imaging (MRI) to determine the brain's mechanisms underlying the symptoms of depression. (© **Scott Camazine/Alamy**)

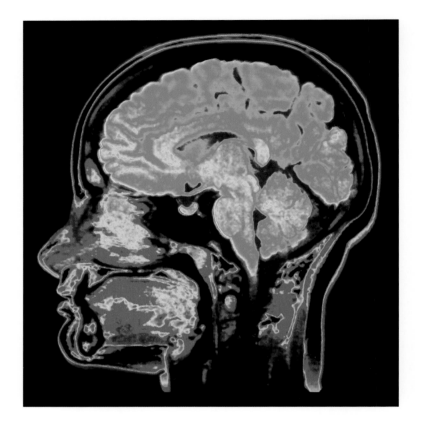

endogenous opioids, or naturally-occurring pain killers. Receptors are specific protein molecules on nerve cells where brain chemicals exert their effect. In a study of 17 untreated patients, the researchers found an overall reduction in the concentration of serotonin 1A receptors in the hippocampus, compared with 19 matched healthy subjects. The hippocampus is a brain region critically involved in memory formation, but also in the regulation of stress, among other functions.

"The reductions in these receptors were correlated with the functional impairment of the patients in work and with their families, with greater impairment being associated with lower receptor concentrations in this region," Zubieta says. Patients responded to treatment with the antidepressant citalopram.

In another study, the scientists examined a subtype of opioid receptor in a separate sample of 18 unmedicated MDD patients. They found that the concentration of "mu" opioid receptors was decreased in the thalamus of these patients, an area implicated in emotion regulation, compared with 19 matched healthy controls. The mu receptors are key molecular switches in regulating mood and triggering brain reward systems.

Exaggerated Stress Responses

These reductions in receptors were further correlated with a greater concentration of stress hormones, such as cortisol, in the blood of the patients, which may reflect an exaggeration of biological stress responses in these patients, say the researchers. They found that patients who failed to respond to the antidepressant fluoxetine (Prozac) had lower concentrations of these specific receptors in the anterior cingulate, a brain area involved in the processing of emotional states.

This information highlights the biological diversity of MD [major depression], Zubieta says. In addition, alterations in brain chemical systems and brain circuitry involved in stress and responses to environmental events can disrupt an individual's work, social, and family life, and response to typical antidepressant treatment. Improved understanding of the sources of this biological diversity, including genetic and environmental influences, will help define subtypes of the illness and their implications for diagnosis and treatment.

"For example, the study on the mu opioid system suggests that a profound dysregulation of central stress-responsive systems may identify a subgroup of patients less likely to respond to first-line, standard antidepressant treatments," Zubieta says. "Further delineation of these processes would lead to the development of tests that may orient treatment decisions. Of course, there are a number of neurotransmitter systems that may be disregulated in

MDD, this being the topic of ongoing research and tool development."

Depressed People Are Prevented from Experiencing Pleasure

In other studies, researchers are using PET and functional magnetic resonance imaging (fMRI) to determine the brain mechanisms underlying one of the symptoms of depression—anhedonia, or the inability to experience pleasure. "The identification of brain systems and circuits whose activity can be correlated with specific symptoms is a first step toward the development of more targeted and effective treatments for depression and other disorders of the brain," says Wayne Drevets, MD, of NIMH. Drevets' review of five studies—involving about 120 patients and as many controls—reveals abnormal patterns of neural activity and brain chemical function in specific circuits in depressed people as they perform reward processing tasks. The series of neuroimaging studies from the NIMH show how abnormalities in their brain reactions during the act of winning money could be turning normal pleasures into unimportant or even uncomfortable events.

In the brain, feelings of pleasure coincide with the release of the chemical dopamine, which is then taken up by proteins called receptors designed to receive it. The network of areas in the brain devoted to processing pleasurable experiences interacts with dopamine to form a "reward-learning pathway," including the amygdala and hippocampus. This network participates more generally in controlling emotional behavior and organizing activities designed to achieve goals, and storing memories.

To test the idea that depressed people's impaired ability to feel and react may be caused by different patterns of responding within the reward-learning pathway, scientists using PET and fMRI looked for differences in brain blood flow, dopamine release, change in mood, and per-

PET Scans Reveal Differences Between Healthy and Depressed Brains

A PET scan can compare brain activity during periods of depression (left) with normal brain activity (right). An increase of blue and green colors, along with decreased white and yellow areas, shows decreased brain activity due to depression.

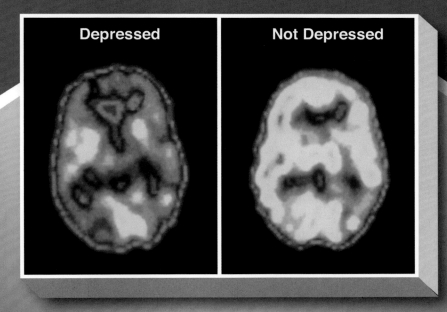

Depressed   **Not Depressed**

formance by participants given a chance to win money. These activities are known to turn on the brain's reward pathway. Tasks ranged in difficulty and level of reward. Half were done without reward; half included a screen after each response telling subjects whether or not they had answered correctly and how much they had won or lost.

"In the end, healthy and depressed people won the same amounts of money, but people in the depressed group still felt bad," says Drevets. "They felt and did worse, in fact, when informed how they were doing. By contrast, such information had no effect on the mood or performance of healthy subjects. In addition, as the subjects received rewards, dopamine was released in the brains of healthy individuals, but not of depressed individuals."

Brain scans revealed that when depressed patients knew that their performance was being tracked and money was on the line, they did worse on the tasks and showed an increase in activity in the amygdala—a brain area known to control the expression of emotions, particularly fear. Activity also rose in the hippocampus and the insula on the left side of the brain. In depressed subjects, the prospect of winning appears to have generated enough anxiety to hamper their performance, especially on the harder tasks.

Brain reactions in the two groups also differed in areas of higher brain function, with depressed subjects showing less activity in the cerebral cortex than healthy subjects. "The relative lack of activity in the seat of reason may mean that depressed people do not apply as much thought as healthy ones to the evaluation of experiences when deciding if they are pleasant or unpleasant, stressful or fun," says Drevets. "Their brains rather seem to pass over the potential pleasure of winning money to focus on unpleasant emotions caused by the potential for failure."

Drevets notes that while much remains to be learned about the biology of depression, these studies contribute to understanding of how a specific symptom, anhedonia, produces abnormal patterns of activity in the brain.

Finding Brain Changes in Youth

In other work, cutting-edge, specialized applications of MRI reveal differences in the brain circuitry of emotions in adults with bipolar disorder (BD), reports Hilary Blumberg, MD, of Yale School of Medicine. MRI images show decreases in the volume of the brain's prefrontal cortex and its subcortical connections sites, including the amygdala in individuals with BD when compared with persons without BD. Functional neuroimaging studies of BD also have demonstrated abnormalities in the functioning of these brain structures, especially during the processing of emotional stimuli and during tasks that require the inhibition of impulsive responses.

The correspondence between the maturation of this circuitry and the emergence of prominent symptoms of BD in adolescence implicate abnormalities in the development of this circuitry during adolescence, says Blumberg. Recent findings of differences in the amygdala in teens with BD suggest brain changes in youth that may help in early detection and that might be targeted for early intervention. Other changes, such as those in prefrontal areas, may also be occurring during the teenage years.

Recent evidence also suggests that treatments may have the potential to reverse the circuitry abnormalities by restoring brain chemical functioning or by repairing circuitry structure through the effects of nerve growth factors. This raises the possibility to intervene early to prevent progression and improve prognosis.

"The findings provide important, new leads that may help in the development of new ways to detect the disorder earlier, to provide more effective treatments, and hopefully to someday prevent the disorder," Blumberg says.

In addition, new methods are being used to assess the integrity of the connections within this emotional brain circuit, such as diffusion tensor imaging and measures of functional connectivity. These have the potential to provide windows onto the connections within the circuitry disrupted in BD. Researchers are also combining genetic studies with imaging studies. "This is exciting as it may help us to identify new treatment strategies aimed at the molecular mechanisms associated with genes that affect brain circuitry," Blumberg says.

FAST FACT

Men produce serotonin, a neurotransmitter that appears to be one of the major players in mood disorders, about 52 percent faster than women do, according to a study published in 1997 in the *Proceedings of the National Academy of Sciences*.

Separating ADHD from Bipolar Disorder

Scientists also are using fMRI to help determine whether children have severe irritability and ADHD [attention deficit/hyperactivity disorder] as opposed to a form of bipolar disorder. This technique appears to separate youth with bipolar disorder from those with chronic irritability—suggesting a way that brain imaging may ultimately be helpful in clinical diagnosis.

"We're finding that these very irritable children with ADHD share some characteristics with children with bipolar disorder, but also have significant differences," says Leibenluft. Very irritable children with ADHD don't have the distinct episodes of mania that one sees in classic bipolar disorder, and they don't tend to have as much bipolar disorder in their family history. However, in a recent study she found that very irritable children with ADHD and those with bipolar disorder both frustrated more easily than controls, and they both had difficulty reading facial emotional cues; they shared deficits in social cognition.

"Yet what's happening in the brain during frustration differed between the two groups," says Leibenluft. "So these data indicate that, even when two groups of patients exhibit the same symptom, the brain mechanisms underlying that symptom can differ. Data like these indicate how, eventually, psychiatric diagnosis will be based on brain mechanisms, in addition to symptoms."

Leibenluft's study of frustration was performed using measures obtained on an electroencephalography machine. Her team is now extending the work by using magnetoencephalography (MEG), a new imaging technique that can detect electrical activity deep in the brain with excellent resolution in terms of both when and where activity takes place. Like MRI technologies, MEG does not involve any radiation or injections, so it is safe and comfortable for children. Using MEG technology, Brendan Rich, PhD, and other members of Leibenluft's team have identified some of the brain regions responsible for the difficulty that children with bipolar disorder have regulating their emotions when frustrated.

Specifically, the researchers found that the anterior cingulate, a region that directs attention to important signals in the environment, functions differently in children with bipolar disorder, compared with healthy children, when they are in frustrating situations. The anterior cingulate acts in concert with the prefrontal cortex, an area that organizes behavior—and here too the researchers found differences between the responses of patients and healthy children. Now, the researchers are conducting a similar study in children with severe irritability and ADHD, to see once again if the brain mechanisms involved in frustration differ between this group and children with bipolar disorder.

Understanding "Epigenetics" and Its Impact on Mood Disorders

James Potash

In the following article James Potash describes the genetic mechanism called "epigenetics" and how it may play a role in mood disorders. Epigenetics is a natural process in which genes are biochemically modified to affect their expression. According to Potash, most genes are epigenetically modified by the addition of methyl groups or histones. Potash explains how he and his research group are investigating whether people with mood disorders have one or more genes that are abnormally modified. That is, the gene may have too many or too few histones or methyl groups attached to it, causing it to be abnormally expressed. Potash is professor of psychiatry and codirector of the Mood Disorders Program at the Johns Hopkins School of Medicine.

Epigenetics is among the hottest topics in medical science today. It is the subject of papers in many of the leading journals and it is a top priority for funding at the National Institutes of Health. And it could turn out to be a big part of the story in depression and bipolar disorder.

SOURCE: James Potash, "Epigenetics Might Provide Clues for Mood Disorders," *ABC News*, May 13, 2008. Courtesy of ABC News.

What Is Epigenetics?

The term [epigenetics] has been around since developmental biologist Conrad Waddington used it in the 1940s to refer to factors that influence how a genetic predisposition will ultimately play out in a biological or clinical outcome.

Now, in the molecular era, the term refers more narrowly to heritable information within cells that is not the DNA sequence itself.

While genetic transmission of information can be thought of as constituted by the chemical letters of the DNA sequence, epigenetic transmission can be considered to reside in the fonts of those letters, and in the punctuation.

The fonts matter. For example, take the sentences, "I hate being depressed," and "I *hate* being depressed." While the words are the same, the second one is a stronger statement. Or take "I *hate* being depressed!!!" Stronger still. Analogously, epigenetic modification of genes plays a major role in how strongly a gene is turned on.

These modifications take two forms: DNA methylation and histone marks.

DNA methylation refers to the addition of a chemical group called a methyl group to places in the DNA sequence. To use another metaphor, these act like locks on the factory door, determining whether chemical workers can come in and turn genes on.

Histones form balls of protein around which DNA wraps. They act like magnets that, when oriented plus to minus, lock the DNA into a closed position, but when oriented plus to plus, repel, and cause the DNA to open up. Various chemical modifications or marks influence the plus vs. minus state and thus help determine whether the doors to the gene are open.

FAST FACT

Approximately 20.9 million American adults, or about 9.5 percent of the population aged eighteen and older in a given year, have a mood disorder, according to a 2005 article in the *Archives of General Psychiatry*.

Researchers use high performance computers to model methylation reactions between DNA and proteins (pictured) to help identify decline in a patient's neurodevelopment. **(Science Source/Photo Researchers, Inc.)**

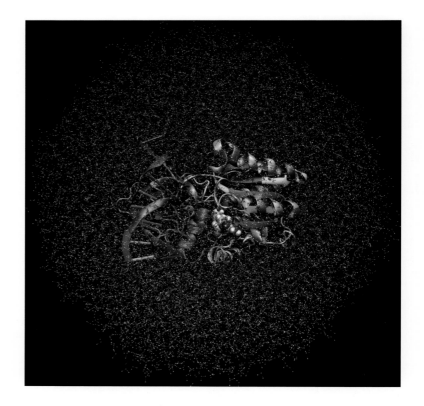

Epigenetics and the Brain

Many cancer genes are known to be regulated by epigenetic machinery, including the colon cancer gene, APC, and the breast cancer gene, BRCA1. But epigenetics has recently been found to play a role in the brain as well.

Our group at Johns Hopkins recently measured DNA methylation levels in hundreds of genes, comparing patterns across three different brain regions. We found that levels differed between regions for many of the genes, suggesting that DNA methylation signatures distinguish brain regions and may help account for the unique roles played by each of the three.

A dramatic example of the role of DNA methylation in brain disease is Rett syndrome, in which a hereditary defect in the DNA methylation machinery leads to a failure to turn off appropriate genes in the brain and a subsequent decline in neurodevelopment for the unfortunate children afflicted with this illness.

However, epigenetic marks can also be altered by the environment. For example, one study showed much greater DNA methylation differences between middle-aged identical twins than between very young ones, suggesting these changes accumulated during the lifetime of the twins.

Might stress be one of the life experiences that influence epigenetic marks?

A fascinating study from McGill University in Montreal suggests the answer could be yes. Researchers showed that in rats, differential maternal behavior towards pups influences their stress sensitivity in adulthood. Pups of better rat mothers showed differences in DNA methylation and histone marks compared to those of less attentive moms at the site of a key stress system gene. Treatment with a drug that changed the epigenetic marks abolished the maternal effect on stress sensitivity, supporting a causal role for epigenetics.

Another study, from the University of Texas Southwestern Medical Center, provides evidence that epigenetic changes can be induced by stress in adulthood. Adult mice exposed to highly aggressive neighbors become socially avoidant, defeated, and subordinate, in some ways mimicking human depression. Researchers showed that these mice developed histone changes in a depression-related gene, and that these changes were reversed by the antidepressant imipramine.

There is evidence that other antidepressants—Parnate and Prozac—can also alter histone marks. And giving mice a histone-altering chemical produces an antidepressant-like effect. One of the leading bipolar disorder medications, valproic acid, influences histones as well.

DNA and Epigenetics

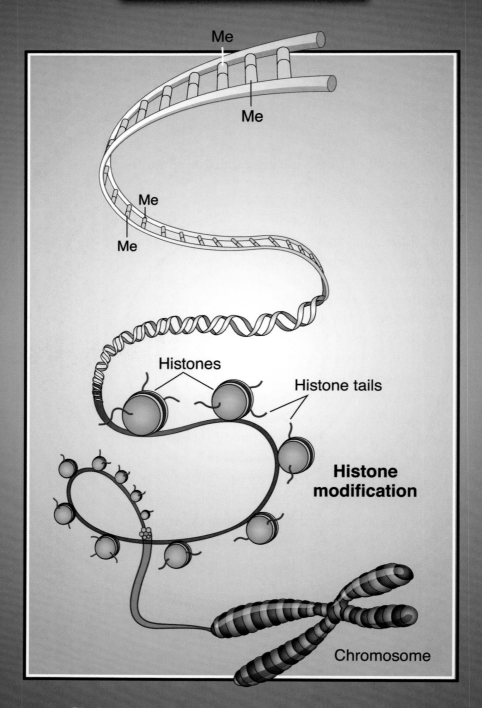

Epigenetics and Mood Disorders

At the Johns Hopkins Epigenetics Center, we are investigating epigenetic variations that might play a role in stress, depression, and bipolar disorder. One of our tools is a microarray, sometimes called a chip, which is about the size of your hand, and has 2.1 million microscopic pieces of DNA on it.

When DNA from a person or a mouse is placed on it, the chip can detect methylation across nearly every gene in the mix, all at the same time. The lead developer of this tool, center director Andrew Feinberg, named it CHARM, an acronym, because Baltimore, where Johns Hopkins is located, has been optimistically dubbed "Charm City."

There is ample reason to be optimistic that advances in our understanding of the epigenetics of mood disorders will ultimately lead to better treatments. As Winston Churchill, who suffered from depression himself, said: "For myself I am an optimist—it does not seem to be much use being anything else."

CHAPTER 2

Controversies About Mood Disorders

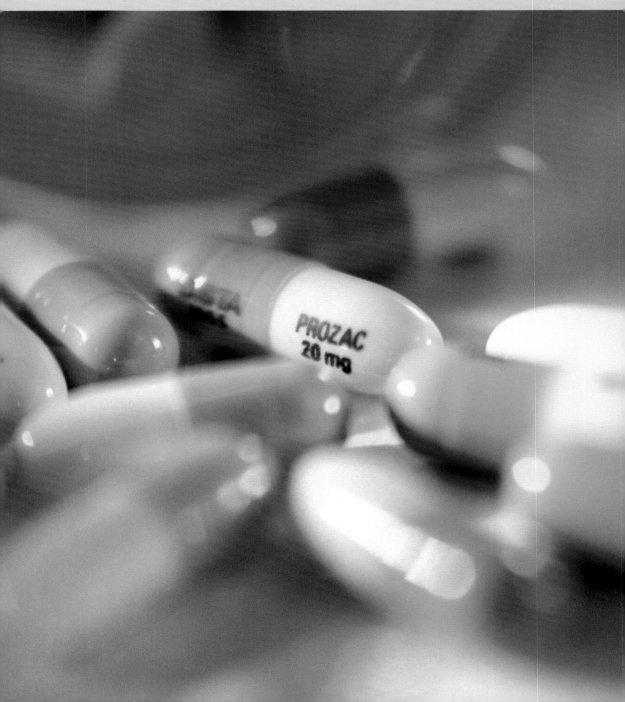

Bipolar Disorder May Be Underdiagnosed

National Institute of Mental Health

In the following viewpoint the National Institute of Mental Health (NIMH) asserts that bipolar disorder is underecognized and improperly treated. According to NIMH researcher Kathleen Merikangas, bipolar disorder is not a single disease. Instead it is a "spectrum disorder" with a range of symptoms. Merikangas says that doctors and psychiatrists are not diagnosing people who are on the milder end of the spectrum. As a result, these people are often given medications that could cause a worsening of their disease and be potentially dangerous. Merikangas says better screening tools are needed to help doctors recognize the symptoms of bipolar disorder. The National Institute of Mental Health is the U.S. government's mental health research agency.

A new study supports earlier estimates of the prevalence of bipolar disorder in the U.S. population, and suggests the illness may be more accurately characterized as a spectrum disorder. It also finds that many people with the illness are not receiving appropriate

Photo on facing page. Controversy has ignited over the use of antidepressants because such medications sometimes cause a worsening of mood disorders. (SuperStock)

SOURCE: "Bipolar Spectrum Disorder May Be Underrecognized and Improperly Treated," National Institute of Mental Health, May 7, 2007. www.nimh.gov.

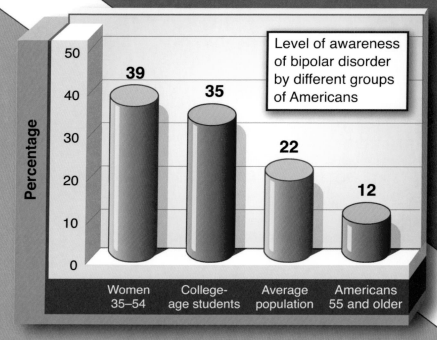

Americans Not Very "Aware" of Bipolar Disorder

Level of awareness of bipolar disorder by different groups of Americans

	Women 35–54	College-age students	Average population	Americans 55 and older
Percentage	39	35	22	12

Taken from: NAMI and Abbott Laboratories survey, Bpkids.org, October 9, 2007.

treatment. The study, published in the May 2007 issue of *Archives of General Psychiatry*, analyzed data from the National Comorbidity Survey Replication (NCS-R), a nationwide survey of mental disorders among 9,282 Americans ages 18 and older. The NCS-R was funded by the National Institutes of Health's National Institute of Mental Health (NIMH).

Unspecified Bipolar Disorder Not Getting Diagnosed

NIMH researcher Kathleen Merikangas, Ph.D., and colleagues identified prevalence rates of three subtypes of bipolar spectrum disorder among adults. Bipolar I is considered the classic form of the illness, in which a person experiences recurrent episodes of mania and depression. People with bipolar II experience a milder form of mania called hypomania that alternates with depressive episodes. People with bipolar disorder not otherwise specified (BD-NOS), sometimes called subthreshold bipolar disorder, have manic and depressive symptoms as well, but they do not meet strict criteria for any specific type of bipolar disorder noted in the *Diagnostic and Statistical Manual for Mental Disorders (DSM-IV)*, the reference manual for psychiatric disorders. Nonetheless, BD-NOS still can significantly impair those who have it.

The results indicate that bipolar I and bipolar II each occur in about 1 percent of the population; BD-NOS occurs in about 2.4 percent of the population. The findings support international studies suggesting that, given its multidimensional nature, bipolar disorder may be better characterized as a spectrum disorder.[1]

"Bipolar disorder can manifest itself in several different ways. But regardless of type, the illness takes a huge toll," said NIMH Director Thomas R. Insel, M.D. "The survey's findings reiterate the need for a more refined understanding of bipolar symptoms, so we can better target treatment."

Most respondents with bipolar disorder reported receiving treatment. Nearly everyone who had bipolar I or II (89 to 95 percent) received some type of treatment, while 69 percent of those with BD-NOS were getting treatment. Those with bipolar I or II were more commonly treated by psychiatric specialists, while those with

> **FAST FACT**
>
> Approximately 41 percent of individuals with an alcohol-use disorder and 60 percent of individuals with a drug-use disorder have a co-occurring mood disorder, according to data from the National Epidemiologic Survey on Alcohol and Related Conditions.

---

1. Spectrum disorders are not single illnesses. Rather, they are many illnesses, with symptoms ranging from mild to severe.

BD-NOS were more commonly treated by general medical professionals.

Inappropriate Treatment

However, not everyone received treatment considered optimal for bipolar disorder. Up to 97 percent of those who had some type of bipolar illness said they had coexisting psychiatric conditions, such as anxiety, depression or substance abuse disorders, and many were in treatment for those conditions rather than bipolar disorder.

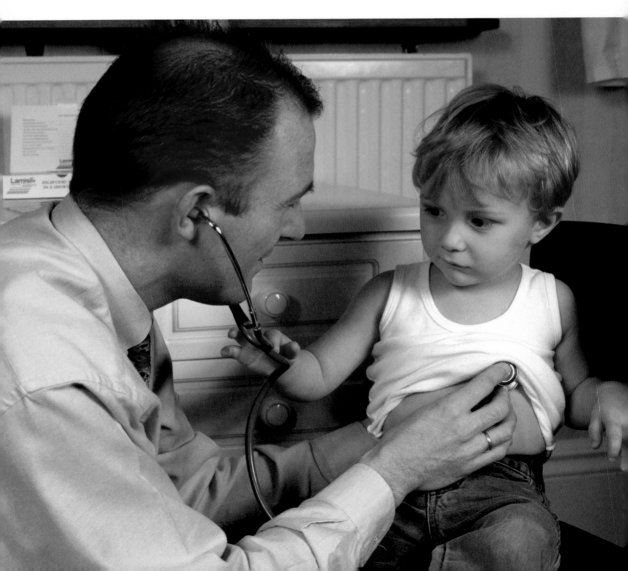

Experts agree that because bipolar disorders often coexist with other illnesses, the former may be underrecognized and undertreated. Better screening techniques are needed. (© Purepix/Alamy)

The researchers found that many were receiving medication treatment considered "inappropriate" for bipolar disorder, e.g., they were taking an antidepressant or other psychotropic medication in the absence of a mood stabilizing medication such as lithium, valproate, or carbamazepine. Only about 40 percent were receiving appropriate medication, considered a mood stabilizer, anticonvulsant or antipsychotic medication.

"Such a high rate of inappropriate medication use among people with bipolar spectrum disorder is a concern," said Dr. Merikangas. "It is potentially dangerous because use of an antidepressant without the benefit of a mood stabilizer may actually worsen the condition."

Need for Better Screening

Merikangas and colleagues speculate that as people seek treatment for anxiety, depression or substance abuse disorders, their doctors, especially if they are not mental health specialists, may not be detecting an underlying bipolar condition in their patients.

"Because bipolar spectrum disorder commonly coexists with other illnesses, it is likely underrecognized, and therefore, undertreated. We need better screening tools and procedures for identifying bipolar spectrum disorder, and work with clinicians to help them better spot these bipolar symptoms," concluded Dr. Merikangas.

Pediatric Bipolar Disorder Is Overdiagnosed

Dov Michaeli

In the following viewpoint Dov Michaeli asserts that there has been an alarming and unjustifiable increase of bipolar disorder diagnoses in children. He thinks that many kids are mistakenly diagnosed with bipolar disorder when in fact they are just stressed and angry because of a lack of parental attention. Michaeli believes the main reason for the excessive number of diagnoses of childhood bipolar disorder is money. Michaeli is an internist and a biotechnology researcher and blogger for The Doctor Weighs In.

O ne of the plays we saw last Sunday in Ashland [Oregon] was *Distracted*, describing a mother whose nine year old child was diagnosed with Attention Deficit Hyperactivity disorder, or ADHD. The kid was a lively, curious, imaginative, highly intelligent child who was bored with his school, couldn't keep his mind concentrated on the dumb and further dumbed down assignments—and was labeled by his teacher as "challenged." It was all downhill from there. The child was seen by all kinds of healers (school nurse, psychologist, neuropsychologist, homeopathic psychiatrist), loaded up with drugs designed to "control" his behavior which in turn led to a new diagnosis: bipolar disorder. I had been vaguely aware of the problems of over-diagnosis and misdiagnosis in child psychiatry, but had no idea of its alarming extent.

The Problem Quantified

In a study published in the September 2007 issue of the *Archives of General Psychiatry* the researchers examined

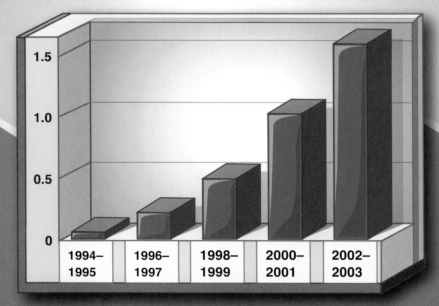

Office Visits for Bipolar Disorder Soaring for the Young

Private doctor's office visits involving a bipolar diagnosis for Americans under twenty, in millions:

Taken from: Benedict Carey, "Bipolar Illness Soars as a Diagnosis for the Young," *New York Times*, September 4, 2007. Source: Mark Olson, Columbia University.

10 years of data from the National Ambulatory Medical Care Survey (NAMCS), an annual, nationwide survey of visits to doctors' offices over a one-week period, conducted by the National Center for Health Statistics. Their finding was astounding.

The researchers estimated that in the United States from 1994–1995, the number of office visits resulting in a diagnosis of bipolar disorder for youths ages 19 and younger was 25 out of every 100,000 people. By 2002–2003, the number had jumped to 1,003 office visits resulting in bipolar diagnoses per 100,000 people. *This is a 40 fold increase in 8 years!* In contrast, for adults ages 20 and older, 905 office visits per 100,000 people resulted in a bipolar disorder diagnosis in 1994–1995; a decade later the number had risen to 1,679 per 100,000 people, a "mere" two fold increase.

About half of all children and adolescents who received a diagnosis of bipolar disorder also received a diagnosis of ADHD.

> **FAST FACT**
>
> Approximately 7 percent of U.S. children are on psychotropic medications, compared to 2.9 percent of Dutch youngsters and 2 percent of German children, according to a 2008 study reported in the journal *Child and Adolescent Psychiatry and Mental Health*.

What Could Account for This Increase?

There could be several factors accounting for this "epidemic."

Increased awareness of the disorder. This may be true to a limited extent, but a sudden awareness by child psychiatrists (90% of the diagnoses were made by them, only 10% by pediatricians) is simply not credible. What were they teaching in medical schools and psychiatry training programs in the decades up to 1995?

Was there a sea change in our knowledge of childhood bipolar disorder since 1995? There has been great progress made in understanding the neurobiology and genetics of the disease. Great progress has been made in drug treatments of psychiatric disorders. But such advances do not affect the diagnosis. The latter is based on observation of behavior, not on objective criteria such as fMRI [functional magnetic resonance imaging] scans of the brain, or biochemical markers of the disease.

The classical manifestation of bipolar disorder is a period of euphoria alternating with deep depression. Yet in children and adolescents euphoria is almost never present. The children are depressed, angry and given to tantrums. But isn't it reasonable to expect a child who is more or less ignored by his harried parents, or is chauffeured from one activity to another, or is subjected to the constant anxiety of Little League and pressure to get the top grades in school, will be angry and depressed? Animal experiments have demonstrated that chronic anxiety, or lack of parental attention, lead to profound depression and aggressive behavior. What makes us think that we are somehow different?

Children and adolescents with bipolar disorder are depressed, angry, and prone to tantrums, but rarely suffer the euphoria adults do. (© Bubbles Photolibrary/Alamy)

I think that the most credible, and most cynical reason for the huge increase in the diagnoses of bipolar disorder and ADHD is money. The diagnosis is made on subjective criteria, and this is an invitation to abuse. I suspect that when this issue will get investigated in depth, it will turn out that psychiatric overdiagnoses are first cousins of excessive cardiac caths, excessive imaging studies, excessive bypass surgeries, excessive prescription of medications, and so on and so on.

I am not a policy wonk, but I sense that this corruption of medicine cannot continue without dire consequences for our society.

Antidepressants Are Not Effective for Treating Depression

Evelyn Pringle

In the following viewpoint Evelyn Pringle contends that antidepressants are ineffective and dangerous, especially for children. Pringle uses quotes and data from several government experts, psychiatrists, scientists, and pharmaceutical industry watchdogs to back up her contention. She maintains that antidepressants are no more effective than placebos, they cause serious side effects, and they increase the risk for suicide. Pringle thinks the off-labeling prescribing of antidepressants to children is particularly reprehensible. Pringle is an investigative journalist. Her essays and opinion pieces can be found at counterpunch.org, opednews.com, and other online sources.

The medicalization of distress has led to a dramatic rise in the use of antidepressants; however, it is questionable whether patients are being told that in controlled clinical trials the drugs barely outperformed a placebo, says Jonathan Leo, Associate Professor of Neuroanatomy, Lincoln Memorial University, DeBusk College of Osteopathic Medicine.

SOURCE: Evelyn Pringle, "Best Kept Secret —SSRIs Do Not Work," LawyersandSettlements.com, March 3, 2007. Reproduced by permission.

Dr Leo also states that patients are not told that in many cases the symptoms of depression will improve within six months even without medication, or that many people have significant physiological problems when they try and get off the drugs. In the interest of informed consent, he notes, patients should be given all the facts before taking an antidepressant.

SSRIs Basically Useless

That said the fact that the class of antidepressants known as the selective serotonin reuptake inhibitors (SSRIs), are basically useless in treating depression in children and adults is not news to the FDA [Food and Drug Administration]. Back on September 23, 2004, during testimony at a hearing before the House Oversight and Investigations Committee on Energy and Commerce, Dr Robert Temple, the FDA's Director of the Office of Medical Policy, discussed the agency's review on the efficacy of SSRIs with the children.

He noted that it was important in a risk-benefit equation to understand the benefit side. "Of the seven products studied in pediatric MDD [major depressive disorder] (Prozac, Zoloft, Paxil, Celexa, Effexor, Serzone and Remeron)," he testified, "FDA's reviews of the effectiveness data resulted in only one approval (Prozac) for pediatric MDD."

"Overall," Dr Temple said, "the efficacy results from 15 studies in pediatric MDD do not support the effectiveness of these drugs in pediatric populations."

Also in 2004, a study of previously hidden unpublished data as well as published studies on five SSRIs, was conducted by Tim Kendall, deputy director of the Royal College of Psychiatrists' Research Unit in London, to help analyze research to draw up the clinical guidelines for British regulators, and published in the *Lancet*.

Following his evaluation, Mr Kendall stated: "This data confirms what we found in adults with mild to moderate depression: SSRIs are no better than placebo, and there is no point in using something that increases the risk of suicide."

In 2005, the *British Medical Journal* published another study that concluded that SSRIs are no more effective than a placebo and do not reduce depression.

Psychiatry for Sale

In December 2006, at the most recent FDA advisory committee meeting held to review studies on SSRI use with adults, SSRI expert, Dr David Healy, author of *The Antidepressant Era*, told the panel that the efficacy of SSRIs has been greatly exaggerated, while the actual studies reveal that only one in ten patients responds specifically to an SSRI rather than a nonspecific factor or placebo.

Critics complain that industry funded studies are presented in ways to exaggerate benefits and obscure side effects. "These include failure to publish negative results, the use of multiple outcome measures, and selective presentation of ones that are positive, multiple publication of positive study results, and the exclusion of subjects from the analysis," according to the paper, "Is Psychiatry for Sale?" by Joanna Moncrieff, in *People's Voice*.

Ms Moncrieff says, psychiatry and the industry make a "formidable combination" because psychiatry derives its legitimacy from the view that mental disorders are equivalent to medical diseases. "Drug treatments that are aimed at specific diagnoses," she explains, "help to endorse this view, and the industry has the financial capacity to ensure that this view becomes accepted and respectable."

"In turn," Ms Moncrieff writes, "the authority of psychiatry enables it to define what is considered as mental disorder and what is appropriate treatment, thus creating markets and opportunities for the pharmaceutical industry."

Pushing Dangerous Pills to Children

Critics are most concerned about the continued profit driven prescribing to children with full knowledge that SSRIs are dangerous and do not work with kids. "Drug companies have targeted children as a big market likely to boost profits and children are suffering as a result, says SSRI expert, psychiatrist Dr Peter Breggin, founder of the International Center for the Study of Psychiatry and Psychology, and author of *Toxic Psychiatry*.

Kelly Patricia O'Meara, author of *Psyched Out: How Psychiatry Sells Mental Illness and Pushes Pills That Kill*, [says that] prescribing SSRIs to kids must stop. "It is unconscionable," she states, "that it even occurs today given the serious warnings recently made mandatory by the FDA."

In the article, "A Prescription for Disaster," pediatrician Lawrence Diller, author of *The Last Normal Child*, notes that child psychiatrists have long been viewed as the authorities in the evaluation and treatment of children's emotional and behavioral problems. "Today, however," he says, "these doctors appear to be pushing pills exclusive of anything else."

As an example, Dr Diller points to a survey of child psychiatry practices by the Yale Child Study Center in the *Journal of the American Academy of Child and Adolescent Psychiatry*, that found that only one in 10 children who visit a child psychiatrist leaves without a prescription.

Child neurologist Dr Fred Baughman, author of *The ADHD Fraud: How Psychiatry Makes Patients of Normal Children*, also says, "pills are invariably prescribed in 91% of the first visits to a child psychiatrist."

According to Dr Baughman, we have 10 million of the 50 million school children in the nation on one or more psychiatric drugs. "This is death by psychiatry," he states.

Off-Label Prescribing Is Dangerous

The FDA approves drugs for uses and with patient populations that have been adequately tested. The term off-label means prescribing a medication for a different patient group, or at a different dose, duration, or combination with another drug, that has not been approved

Critics of the use of SSRIs to treat children say that drug companies are more interested in profits than in the effectiveness of the drugs and that children are suffering as a result. (© Rob Walls/Alamy)

as safe and effective. While doctors may legally prescribe a drug for an unapproved use, drug makers are barred from promoting a drug for off-label uses but it's common knowledge that they do it on a regular basis.

The cost of off-label prescribing has become a major health problem in the US. According to the 2006 report, *Preventing Medication Errors*, by the Institute of Medicine, each year errors in the way drugs are prescribed, delivered and used, injure 1.5 million people in the hospital setting alone and cost more than $3.5 billion a year to treat.

Medical experts warn that prescribing drugs to children that have been approved only for adults, is extremely dangerous because the correct dosage has not been established for their weight and developing body organs. According to patient rights activist, Doyle Mills, psychiatry is turning into Russian Roulette. "There is no known safe dose," he says, "for any of these psychiatric drugs in young children. They are never tested in the under-five population," Mr Mills says, "yet children can be given these drugs legally."

California attorney Ted Chabasinski, who handles cases involving patient rights and exposing the off-label marketing of psychiatric drugs, says, "the drug companies, and their subsidiary, the American psychiatric profession, push drugs for children that have never been shown to be beneficial, but clearly are dangerous and have many life-threatening effects."

According to Vera Sharav, Director of the Alliance for Human Research Protections, "The only way to stop the prescribed assault on America's children is to put health care professionals (mostly psychiatrists) who prescribe toxic psychotropic drugs (and drug cocktails) for children—for whom these drugs have not been approved as either safe or effective—on trial in open court."

FAST FACT

According to a 2008 study reported in the *New England Journal of Medicine,* published literature suggests that antidepressants are effective 94 percent of the time. However, when unpublished data are considered, antidepressants are effective only 51 percent of the time.

"Let the public bear witness," she states, "to the proceedings that will demonstrate the absence of scientific-medical evidence to support the widespread misprescribing of harmful drugs for children."

SSRIs Cause Dangerous Side Effects

Evidence from many sources confirms that SSRIs commonly cause or exacerbate a wide range of abnormal mental and behavioral conditions, according to Dr Breggin. "These adverse drug reactions," he states, "include the following overlapping clinical phenomena: a stimulant profile that ranges from mild agitation to manic psychoses, agitated depression, obsessive preoccupations that are alien or uncharacteristic of the individual, and akathisia [restlessness]."

Each of these reactions, he explains, can worsen the individual's mental condition and can result in suicidality, violence, and other forms of extreme abnormal behavior.

SSRIs have been on the market less than 20 years so their long-term effects are still unknown. Barry Tuner, a professor of law and medical ethics in the UK [United Kingdom], says mental illness has skyrocketed in the US because drug companies have marketed it and the US is facing a "societal catastrophe" if this is not reined in.

"In twenty years," he warns, "a huge percentage of the population will be damaged by these medications and the recipients will have real mental disorders caused by the drugs."

Studies are being conducted in [an] attempt to assess the long-term damage on kids. Last year [2006], Dr Amir Raz, assistant professor in the Division of Child and Adolescent Psychiatry at Columbia University, and researcher at the New York State Psychiatric Institute, writing in the journal *PLoS Medicine*, said mouse studies indicate exposure to SSRIs early in life produces abnormal emotional behaviors in adults.

"Some exploratory findings," Dr Raz wrote, "suggest that artificial perturbation of serotonin function in early life may alter the normal development of brain systems related to stress, motor development, and motor control."

Other medical experts warn that the harm caused to the body by psychiatric drugs is not limited to mental disorders. Dr Grace Jackson, author of *Rethinking Psychiatric Drugs: A Guide for Informed Consent*, points out that, "some physicians seem to only think these pills affect everything from the neck up, and they forget that

"Side effects may include loss of appetite, job, home and family," cartoon by Mike Baldwin. www.CartoonStock.com.

when they give the medications there is an entire human body that may be feeling unanticipated effects of these medications."

Most patients, including parents acting on behalf of their children, know little if anything about off-label pre- scribing and assume that their doctors are giving them an approved drug for an approved use. But all too often, experts say, through no fault of their own, patients wind up with more serious health problems than they had to begin with due to off-label prescribing.

Antidepressants Can Be Harmful for People with Bipolar Disorder

Brenda Patoine

In the following viewpoint Brenda Patoine asserts that many psychiatrists are concerned about the misuse of antidepressants for the treatment of bipolar disorder. According to Patoine, antidepressants can trigger manic episodes in people with bipolar disorder, and the medications should be used only as a last resort. Unfortunately, says Patoine, many doctors are prescribing antidepressants to treat bipolar disorder. Additionally, many bipolar patients receive antidepressants when their bipolar disorder is misdiagnosed as major depression. According to Patoine, while many people are focusing on antidepressants' suicide risk, the bigger concern is the misuse of these drugs to treat bipolar disorder. Patoine is a science writer who has been covering neuroscience for more than fifteen years.

The question of whether some prescription medications, particularly antidepressants, increase the risk of suicide has stirred great debate, but some experts in psychiatry lament that the continued emphasis on this extremely rare event has deflected attention from

SOURCE: Brenda Patoine, "Antidepressant Debate May Miss the Mark," *BrainWork*, May 1, 2008. Copyright © 2008 The Dana Foundation. All rights reserved. Reproduced by permission.

matters of greater clinical relevance. Of particular concern are side effects such as agitation and mania that are often the result of inappropriate use of antidepressants in people with bipolar disorder.

Suicide Issue "Blown Out of Proportion"

The current debate with respect to suicide risk erupted in 2004, when the Food and Drug Administration [FDA] required drug makers to place a "blackbox" warning on the pills' labels to reflect data suggesting increased rates of suicidal thinking among adolescents.

In the wake of the action there has been both outrage and applause, and opinions on the subject from mental health experts tend to be strong. Fred Goodwin, a former director of the National Institute of Mental Health who is now director of a research center at George Washington University, called the 2004 black-box warning "the worst example of regulatory overreach" he has seen.

Tom Insel, current director of the National Institute of Mental Health, is more cautious: "Has the black box done more harm? The jury is still out," he says, citing conflicting research findings.

Robert Post, former chief and 36-year veteran of the National Institute of Mental Health's Biological Psychiatry Branch, says that the publicity after the FDA decision largely ignored the complexities of the issue and left many people with the false idea that antidepressants cause suicide. "The suicide issue has been totally blown out of proportion," he says.

Bipolar Mistreatment and Misdiagnosis a Bigger Problem

Post, Goodwin and other mental health experts say a far greater concern centers on the use of antidepressants in bipolar disorder. Bipolar is characterized by mood swings from depression to states of mania or hypomania

Treating Bipolar Disorders with Antidepressants May Cause Harm

Effects of Antidepressants

Ten to twenty percent of bipolar patients cycle into mania.	Twenty percent of patients experience more frequent episodes and a worsening of their bipolar disorder.

Taken from: S. Nassir Ghaemi, "Prescribing Antidepressants for Depression in Bipolar Disorder—Point/Counterpoint," *Psychiatric Times*, August 1, 2004.

(literally, "below" mania), in which the person may feel a range of possible symptoms including heightened energy, racing thoughts and less need for sleep. The manic phase differentiates bipolar illness from "unipolar" depression, which is also known as major depression or recurrent depression.

Bipolar is often misdiagnosed and treated as unipolar depression, particularly in general practices but even among psychiatric specialists. One reason, Goodwin says, is because people with the disorder are far more likely to seek medical help during a depressed period than during a manic period, and clinicians do not always uncover a history of manic symptoms.

"The biggest issue is the problem of improper diagnosis," says Post. "There are more than a half-dozen studies around the world indicating that if you do careful diagnostic assessments of people diagnosed with recurrent unipolar depression, you find that about 30 to 40 percent of the people who are being treated as depressives actually have bipolar disorder. These people are at extraordinarily greater risk for switching into mania."

Post says it is clear from research that antidepressants can induce agitated states or outright mania in someone who has an underlying vulnerability to bipolarity, such as a previous manic episode or a family history of manic or hypomanic behavior. But these histories are notoriously difficult to nail down in the real world of time-constrained general-medicine practices.

"If the clinician doesn't insist on talking with a relative, then half the diagnoses for bipolar are going to be missed," says Goodwin, who coauthored the definitive medical textbook on bipolar disorder with Kay Redfield Jamison. Studies suggest that even among people who have been hospitalized for mania, up to 60 percent do not report the episodes to their clinicians.

"If clinicians don't recognize a patient is bipolar and they think they're treating a unipolar patient, often they only find out they're treating a bipolar when the treatment [with an antidepressant] brings out the bipolarity," Goodwin says. "They may have actually created bipolarity. It's a step you can't take back, because once a person has had a manic episode they're likely to have more, even without the antidepressant."

FAST FACT

Approximately 60 percent of patients with bipolar disorder have attempted suicide, according to data reported on the government's National Quality Measures Clearinghouse Web site.

Antidepressants Only a Last Resort

Goodwin is not willing to see a depressed patient for evaluation or treatment unless a family member is present in the interview process, which he says is quickly becoming the standard of care at mood disorder clinics affiliated with major academic hospitals.

Even among people who are correctly diagnosed as bipolar, research indicates that close to half are being treated with antidepressants without a mood-stabilizing drug such as lithium or newer antipsychotic drugs, a situation

In a recent study, the Texas Algorithm, experts recommend using antidepressants only as a last resort if other mood-stabilizing drugs do not work.
(© Jaubert Bernard/Alamy)

that "everyone agrees is inappropriate and is going to lead to problems with switching," Post says.

The most recent expert consensus report designed to guide the treatment of bipolar disorder, dubbed the Texas Algorithm, recommends using antidepressants only as a last resort if other combinations of mood stabilizers don't work. "In the eyes of the experts, antidepressants have been demoted [in bipolar treatment]," says Goodwin. "But still, in clinical practice, the most likely thing to happen when the patient is depressed is that they will end up on an antidepressant."

There are signs that the inappropriate use of antidepressants in bipolar disorder is actually changing the characteristics of the disease. "We know that bipolar illness has gotten worse since the explosion in the use of antidepressants," Goodwin says. His hunch is that the trend is related to how many bipolar patients are on antidepressants, since the drugs are known to induce switching to manic states or to induce more rapid "cycling" between depression and mania.

"I think the advice is, pay attention to antidepressants for the real reasons, like the increased agitation and mania that can occur. If these drugs had a label that said: 'Before using an antidepressant, you must screen for bipolarity and include a family member in the screening process,' that would be a really helpful label."

He adds: "Unfortunately, we got distracted by this suicidality silliness."

Antidepressants Can Safely Be Used to Treat Bipolar Disorder

Simon Sobo

In the following viewpoint Simon Sobo contends that antidepressants can be safely used to treat bipolar disorder. According to Sobo, concerns about antidepressants triggering episodes of mania are overblown. Sobo thinks doctors should be more concerned about giving bipolar patients another group of medications—mood stabilizers. He believes mood stabilizers are "downers," and he thinks downers are not always appropriate treatments for bipolar disorder or depression. Sobo also thinks bipolar disorder is overdiagnosed. Sobo is director of psychiatry at New Milford Hospital in Connecticut.

T he definitions of "mood swings" and "mood stabilizers" have been radically changed since their original usage. Mood swings, in bipolar disorder, originally referred to the changes from mania (highs) to lows (depressions) and vice-versa that occurred in the course of manic-depression. Rapid cycling mood swings

SOURCE: Simon Sobo, "Summary of Bipolar Disorder Article and Additions Since It Was Written," simonsobo.blogspot.com, March 22, 2005. Reproduced by permission of the author.

were defined as *4 changes in a year*. Mood stabilizers were supposed to be drugs that were both antidepressants and anti-manic agents. There was, what I will call, a sentimental belief that mood stabilizers might get at the basic cause of the disease, and over the long term, prevent worse and worse rapid cycling. This reasoning was somewhat like good control of diabetes where it was hoped close monitoring might prevent later problems like diabetic induced blindness. Applied to "mood stabilizers" use in manic depression, it is a great idea if correct, but it is at best a guess. It has never been shown to actually happen, even in unequivocally diagnosed bipolar patients. We simply don't know.

Mood Stabilizers Are "Downers"

Moreover, the basic cause of the disease is not known and each of the "mood stabilizers" work in completely different ways. So there is no reason to think that any one of these drugs, or many of them used simultaneously, are curing the illness (as say, penicillin cures strep throat by killing streptococcus bacteria). It is more accurate to think of them as medications to help control symptoms, not a trivial accomplishment, but this is relevant if the "symptoms" are not creating a problem (such as some forms of hypomania). Essentially, as might be expected, most of the "mood stabilizers" are downers. They slow down neuronal discharges, about what you would expect from anti-seizure medication. Consistent with what they do, they also may be used in other conditions in which we might imagine incredibly active neurons firing away, e.g. people with explosive disorder (who fly into uncontrollable rages) people with panic disorder (where patients describe extreme terror) as well as mania. There is no basis for calling them mood stabilizers. Anti-manic drugs is more appropriate. A common side effect is what might be expected, somnolence, lack of energy, sleeping a lot.

Bipolar II: Bipolar Disorder Without Mania

One study of 13 classical bipolar I patients found that when their moods were measured every 2 hours, 5 of them had moods all over the map—high, low, what have you. This was not a discovery. It has always been recognized that bipolar patients can present with a "mixed" picture. What was a big deal was that these authors speculated that these mood changes represented "ultra rapid cycling." This idea went completely unchallenged, even though there was no particular basis for this concept. Even more striking, the idea was embraced by many psychiatrists, particularly because another change in thinking had taken place regarding how we should define bipolar disorder. The idea of bipolar II came into being. It was possible to have bipolar disorder without ever being manic.

Diagnosing some people who have never been manic to, nevertheless, have bipolar disorder, is reasonable. Many genetic diseases have incomplete penetrance, meaning some people have a gene for an illness, but for whatever reason, they don't have the full illness. It is valid to assume this happens with bipolar disorder and keep this is mind when treating with antidepressants as they might send patients into a full manic episode. The problem is, that once "hypomania" became a criterion, it was so loosely defined that all kinds of patients might qualify, whether their hypomania was representative of an illness or not. Moreover, with this expanded use of the term "mood swings" patients with labile [changing] moods were being told they have mood swings and therefore were bipolar II. The phenomenon was so widespread that I decided to write my article, but so far there has been almost no discussion of this issue in the literature despite the radical shift in thinking that took place.

Bipolar II opened up a can of worms. All kinds of moody people, people with bad tempers, impulsive people, adolescents with poorly formed identities and labile moods, drug abusers, irritable people, and finally moody children were, and are, being assigned a bipolar diagnosis. *Time* magazine ran a cover story on "bipolar children." Many people use newspapers, and news magazines and TV for health information. This is very unfortunate. In this case the story was written by a young reporter who admitted to me that she didn't know that much about manic depression. She had only been working on the story for a few weeks. Reporters, such as her, might draw as her next assignment a story on bananas. This story, and an Oprah book [a book featured on Oprah Winfrey's talk show], gave the impression that medicine had to be given to these kids early to keep the illness from "progressing."

The other reason I wrote my article was that this diagnosis was often made by doctors at inpatient units after a suicide attempt by a moody or impulsive teenager. The psychiatrists who made the diagnosis had spent, in total, less than an hour with the patient. I would then see them as an outpatient when they were discharged and they were already complaining about enormous weight gain and the desire to sleep 14–16 hours a day. They, and their families, were convinced that they had to take the medicine for life in order to correct their "chemical imbalance." Bipolar patients can, and often do have labile moods, but so do many other conditions, that are not necessarily related to bipolar disorder, and should not be the basis for making the diagnosis, as appears to have happened. Furthermore, there is no particular reason to believe that "mood stabilizers" should be particularly helpful here even though the term implies it should be exactly what is needed. To reiterate, many "mood stabilizers" are depressants. They slow you down, a characteristic that makes them useful for mania, anxiety and other states of high excitement (including epilepsy, their original reason for being on the market).

Overdiagnosis Means Too Many People on Mood Stabilizers

Some "bipolar II" patients will turn out to have bipolar disease. A good number of them won't. Vanessa Grigoria addressed this issue in a cover story in *New York* magazine [titled] "Are You Bipolar?" She had noticed that many of her young and foolish friends in Manhattan were being told that they had bipolar disorder by doctors, who saw them every few months for 15 minutes, meaning they *wouldn't* eventually mature and regret their young wild ways. The diagnosis of bipolar disorder meant they would have this disease for life. They were not too thrilled that their drug induced lethargic behavior and thinking had grown to resemble the oldish doctors who made the diagnosis.

In addition to sloppy arguments about the nature of bipolar disorder there are many reasons for what I am claiming is the overdiagnosis of this and many other conditions. I think the problem is *DSM IV* [*Diagnostic and Statistical Manual of Mental Disorders, 4th Edition*] or at least the paradigm that has grown around it. I attack this notion in several of my articles. Not too long ago, it was believed that a secret to be revealed in the course of psychoanalysis, a forgotten event might free a patient of his or her symptoms. The same thing has happened with *DSM IV* diagnosis. Clinicians, family members, patients believe that if only the *real* diagnosis can be discovered, then an explanation will be available that explains the illness. Aha it was a cancer all along, or Lupus, or Lyme disease, or whatever. "Now we can treat it." A person may not appear to be obviously manic, or ADHD [having attention deficit/hyperactivity disorder], or autistic (a topic I will address in the future) or whatever, but if we can make the correct *diagnosis* the problem is solved. The mystery is over. How this kind of

FAST FACT

Approximately 11 percent of patients received four or more antidepressants *before* they were diagnosed with bipolar disorder, according to a study reported in a 2006 *Medscape General Medicine* article.

categorization can get in the way of good treatment, or even thinking cogently about a particular patient's problems, is the subject of many of my articles. [American psychologist Abraham] Maslow's observation should be added. "If the only tool you have is a hammer, you tend to see every problem as a nail." Many psychiatrists have almost exclusively become medication doctors. The results of this practice follow. Give it a name and give it a drug. And if that doesn't work a different drug, or several different drugs.

I am not against the use of medication, even medication given when a diagnosis cannot be determined. Some of the drugs that have appeared in the last few years are fantastic, offering hope, and better than that, very satisfying results. However, I am against the self deception and deception of the public that "scientific" logic is being used by "experts" to describe what doctors are

Some experts say that psychiatrists tend to overdiagnose bipolar disorder, possibly because medical science has not yet determined the underlying causes of the disorder.
(© WoodyStock/Alamy)

doing. True science will come to psychiatry when we understand the mechanisms behind the symptoms we are treating, and prove that the treatments we are using work. We do not have to apologize, nor should we be blamed for our state of ignorance. We can only know what is known. But this means we have to do a lot of guessing, hopefully *educated* guessing, because we have to try our best and sometimes drugs are quite helpful, when established through this trial and error approach to them.

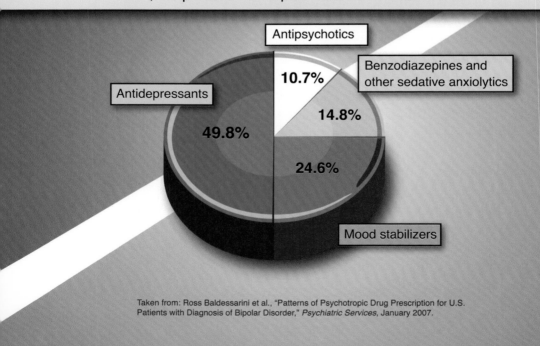

Antidepressants Are the Most Common First Drug Prescribed for Bipolar Disorder in the United States

First prescription given to treat bipolar disorder in a study of 7,760 persons with bipolar disorder in 2002–2003:

Antipsychotics

Benzodiazepines and other sedative anxiolytics

10.7%

14.8%

Antidepressants

49.8%

24.6%

Mood stabilizers

Taken from: Ross Baldessarini et al., "Patterns of Psychotropic Drug Prescription for U.S. Patients with Diagnosis of Bipolar Disorder," *Psychiatric Services*, January 2007.

Antidepressants Have an Important Role to Play

When my article was written the consensus of "experts" was that mood stabilizers should be used as the first treatment for bipolar depressed patients and antidepressants used only as a last resort. There were reasonable concerns about sending depressed patients into mania. But this caution went too far. It was being issued as state of the art treatment despite the fact that no mood stabilizers had been shown to work for depression. On the contrary all the evidence pointed to their usefulness for mania alone. I was completely bewildered by this, especially since the vast majority of psychiatrists like me, doctors in practice spending most of their time treating patients, used antidepressants and the experts were condemning the only treatment we could offer. Indeed Dr. [Jeffrey] Sachs at Harvard had been given a $28 million grant in the hopes of trying to educate non-experts like me and other clinicians in the hinterlands to follow the experts like him. The discrepancy in practice between the experts and us dummies was not mysterious. I had learned when, as chief of the psychiatry at my local hospital, I would try to reach experts to give a talk at our hospital. I had great difficulty getting through to them. They were almost always out of town at conferences, or giving talks. Hence the mystery of their reason for advocating mood stabilizers as the mainstay of treatment was clear. Compared to us they had comparatively little actual contact with patients. So they weren't confronted by the evidence, the failure of their recommended treatment (using drugs such as Depakote and other "mood stabilizers" to treat bipolar depression). Fortunately by 2002 the facts eventually won out. Anti-depressants were granted an important role to play in bipolar depression in revised protocols. It was admitted that previous warnings about their danger may have been overstated.

CHAPTER 3

Personal Stories About Mood Disorders

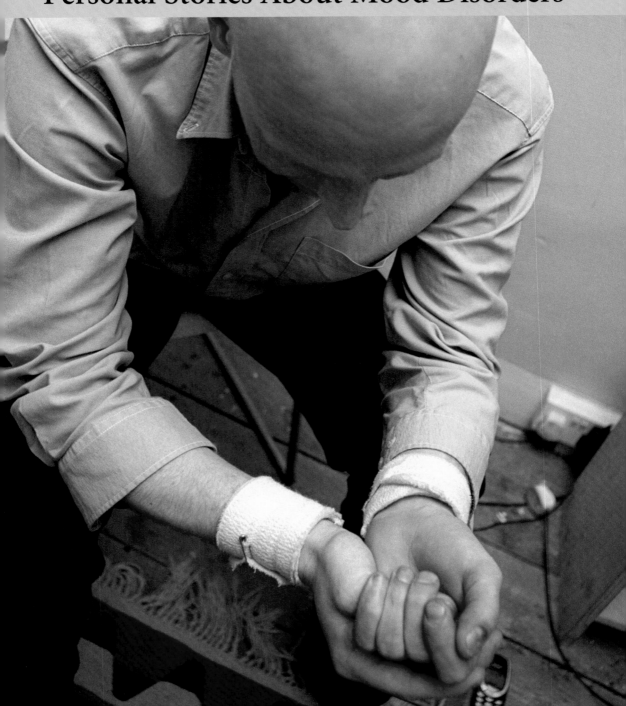

The Day I
Broke Down

Valeria Godines

In the following article *Orange County Register* reporter Valeria Godines reveals what it is like to go insane, be diagnosed with bipolar disorder, and be treated with electroshock therapy. On December 5, 2004, Godines lost touch with reality and was taken to the emergency room of her local hospital. She was hallucinating and believed she had harmed her young daughter Gabriela. In her story Godines takes the reader with her as she recounts her struggle with bipolar disorder—from the mental ward at the hospital, to electroshock therapy treatments, and group therapy sessions. According to Godines, she contemplated suicide several times, but the thought of Gabriela prevented her from going through with it. With the support of her husband, the help of group therapy sessions, and treatment with several medications, including Prozac, Wellbutrin, Lamictal, and Abilify, Godines was able to return to full-time work at *The Orange County Register* a little over a year after her breakdown.

Photo on facing page. People who suffer from mood disorders are often depressed and may find it a struggle simply to get up in the morning. (© Janine Wiedel Photolibrary/ Alamy.)

SOURCE: Valeria Godines, "Five Part Series on Her Battle with Bipolar Disorder," *Orange County Register,* July 9–12, 2006. Copyright © 2006 Orange County Register. Reproduced by permission.

On Dec. 5, 2004, I killed my daughter—Valeria Godines goes completely insane. Police arrive at her house.

I murdered my daughter. My little Gabriela.

The lights move in and out of focus. My heart pounds as I pace up and down, up and down. My little girl. My little Gabriela. I can't breathe fast enough. I can't speak fast enough.

"My father-in-law poisoned me. My husband is really my brother. Wait a minute. I'm a hermaphrodite. Don't you understand? Don't you understand? They're testing me; they're testing me."

I run into the bathroom, sit down on the footstool with the secret compartment where my daughter hides her stuffed lamb. I stare at the white tiles and drop my head into my trembling hands.

I hurt my daughter. My little Gabriela.

I shoot into the bedroom, pick up the phone and dial 911.

I absolutely must confess what I've done.

My husband, David, picks up the other line in the kitchen and frantically tries to interrupt the dispatcher. Four minutes later, the police are at our door.

I know where I need to go.

To jail.

It is Dec. 5, 2004, and I have lost my mind. My husband tells the police that nothing I have said today makes sense.

She loves dinosaurs and books. Gabriela, 3, has cheeks like little pillows and soft, curly brown hair with golden streaks. She mispronounces "Elmo" as "Elbow" and loves to count in Spanish.

My husband, David Fitzgerald, is a brainy college professor who reads *The Economist* but also loves "The Simpsons." He's gorgeous. Loves to cook and travel. He's also incredibly kind, a man who donates to Oxfam and gave my diabetic cat, Pumpkin, insulin shots twice a day.

I love my job at *The Orange County Register,* where I cover Latino issues, write features and frequently report from Mexico. I've written many stories in 19 years in this business, but this is the most personal and important and difficult and painful.

What happened to me was like turbulent weather inside my head. Black became three shades darker; red became blood. I could smell flowers in the next room. I felt primal fear, cornered, as if something ominous were after me.

On Dec. 5, everything was put in jeopardy. My freedom. My life. Even my memories.

My brainstorm shocked many people, including myself. I am not fragile. My co-workers would tell you that I'm aggressive on stories. I roll my eyes at people who have "nervous breakdowns."

Or I used to anyway.

Is it possible to just suddenly go crazy? Or was I born this way? I don't know, but when I turn my reporter's eye on myself, it seems as if it was building up all along.

25 Years Before the Breakdown

I'm getting ready for my First Communion. My white dress scratches my legs. It's stiff, and my polished shoes are too tight. Yet, I feel like a little princess.

I'm 7, and I kneel in the confessional box, making the sign of the cross.

I don't tell the priest how I swore on the playground or stuck my chewing gum under the classroom desk.

No, my sin is far worse.

"Bless me, Father, for I have sinned. I committed adultery."

One of my relatives hurts me with his finger.

Silence fills the box.

Making a sign of the cross, he gives me five Hail Marys and parting advice. He tells me to be sure to hug the man who hurts me.

And tell him that I love him.

23 Years Before the Breakdown

I'm 9 and at my grandparents' house in South Texas, where we're living because my father lost his job. I'm at the piano, touching the keys. I want to learn how to play. Suddenly, I can feel my grandfather staring at me, even though I can't see him.

I know what he wants. He wants to do what he did to me yesterday: fondle me, kiss me. He likes to hunt me, stalk me. I suddenly feel as if I'm freezing, even though it's more than 90 degrees outside.

Between the ages of 7 and 10, I was sexually abused by my grandfather and two other male relatives.

As a child, I fended off my fears with a small, chipped, plastic statue of Jesus. Every night, I clutched it in my hand, praying that nobody would visit me in the dark.

Sometimes my prayers were answered. Sometimes they weren't.

14 Years Before the Breakdown

Wearing my ridiculously high white heels and strapless dress, I tried not to fall as I walked across the floor to accept the award at my senior prom in 1990.

Most Likely to Succeed.

It was just a certificate, really. But it reassured me, because deep down I always thought I would fail. I curled up in a ball on my bedroom floor, crying for hours. I gorged on white bread in the middle of the night. I furiously wrote about the sexual abuse in my journal.

Yes, I had been class president, a popular athlete, the editor of the school paper.

But I often felt my brain sliding sideways, my throat closing. I didn't know there was a name for what was happening to me.

The certificate was a vote of confidence. It gave me hope.

12 Years Before the Breakdown

A picture ran in *The Daily Texan,* the student newspaper at the University of Texas at Austin.

The police are dragging a crazy, homeless woman to a patrol car. She fights them, straining and pulling. Another woman holds out a cigarette for her, and the crazy woman leans toward it, face pained, to take a last puff. As if she were going to be executed.

The man who took that picture must have loved that woman, even if just for a moment. He paid attention to her. Took her seriously. He showed the depths of her pain. He made me look at the moment the way she did. She didn't seem that crazy at all.

I studied the photo caption. By David Fitzgerald.

Later, when I began working at the *Texan*, a handsome, blond photographer walked into the newsroom.

He stuck out his hand.

"Hi. I'm David."

I caught my breath.

"I know who you are."

10 Years Before the Breakdown

We started dating during my senior year when David moved to California, where he wanted to pursue a Ph.D. in sociology. My colleagues at the *Texan* would have told you I was the most put-together person in the newsroom.

But a part of me was still sliding, sliding down.

I needed to get help.

Before it was too late.

I stared at the university psychiatrist and waited for him to finish arguing on the phone. He slammed the receiver down and cursed before looking at me.

"Hey, are you OK?" I asked timidly.

He looked at me in disbelief, as if to say, "Let's remember who is crazy here."

I told him about mental illness in my family: The grandfather who molested me committed suicide; a great aunt was hospitalized with paranoia; another aunt had electroshock.

He prescribed Prozac. It hadn't been on the market long and was being called a wonder drug, appearing on the cover of news magazines.

The psychiatrist promised Prozac would help. I later learned that it works by altering the brain's use of serotonin, which is believed to help regulate mood.

He didn't tell me about the side effects, which include anxiety, sleeplessness and loss of appetite.

The drug seemed to work. I trimmed down, which thrilled me since I've always struggled with my weight. I never slept. I had no appetite. A nervous energy propelled me.

It worked wonders.

David called me every night from Southern California. I told him all about the sexual abuse, which infuriated him. He comforted me, flying out to visit me every month, bringing flowers, handwritten poems and artistic photos. Each meal he prepared was special. Basil steaks, tabouli salad, champagne and homemade pies.

He did my laundry, cleaned my apartment, read my newspaper stories and had fresh coffee waiting for me when I walked through the door. I had to marry this guy.

He got a depressed fiancée, and I got to move to California.

We married in 1997, and I eventually got a job at the *Register*. I had great assignments in Mexico and was being groomed for bigger things.

Things were so good, David and I decided to work on our next dream: a baby.

2 Years Before the Breakdown

The minute I saw her, I fell in love. She was a cashew with a tiny beating heart on the ultrasound screen.

I'll never forget Nov. 17, 2002. She was born shrieking and wailing. A nurse carried her to me, and I nuzzled her, kissed her soft little head and whispered, "I love you."

> **FAST FACT**
>
> Approximately 83 percent of people with bipolar disorder experience a seriously disabling episode, according to data from the National Comorbidity Survey Replication Study.

Gabriela fell silent, as if she recognized my voice, recognized me, the woman who had carried her all those months.

My happiness wouldn't last.

A couple of weeks later, postpartum depression left me sobbing in the bathtub while colicky Gabriela screamed endlessly. I was afraid to hold her, afraid I'd drop her. My dream of breast-feeding dissolved. I lay in bed while David handled everything—bottle feeding, diaper changing, baths, dinner, his dissertation.

Suicidal, I made several phone calls to therapists who told me they weren't accepting new patients. I finally found one who sounded quite kind on the phone and could see me immediately. When I told him I had postpartum depression, he assured me that everything would be all right. That this was all hormonal.

He fell asleep during the session. When he woke with a start, he asked me in a thick voice if I had children.

So much for one-on-one sessions. I'd be better off on meds, I decided.

Another doctor put me on a higher dose of Prozac than I'd been taking before, and for a few months I felt normal. But I weaned myself off it without telling the doctor.

I felt so good, what could be the harm?

I was thrilled to return to work. There, I felt confident. But I was still unsure at home.

I feared that I'd hold Gabriela wrong and break her neck, or lose her in a crowd. I left all baby care to David.

18 Months Before the Breakdown

Things kept getting better at work. In 2003, David was awarded a Fulbright fellowship to study in Mexico. The *Register* assigned me to work as a correspondent there. Everything seemed perfect.

During our year and a half there, I wrote stories that showed links between Orange County and the states of Jalisco and Michoacán. I also worked with a team investigating lead in Mexican candy. The series became a finalist for a Pulitzer Prize.

To help juggle all this, we hired Kika Aguirre, a neighbor, to take care of Gabriela. She fed her, clothed her, played with her, soothed her.

It made me furiously jealous. I could tell that Gabriela loved her. She would imitate Kika, wagging her baby finger just the way Kika did. When Kika and I were in the same room, Gabriela would go to her.

But I couldn't stop myself from letting Kika handle the whole load.

In a small way, I felt justified. After all, I worked full time. I didn't have Gabriela in day care, I reasoned. I could check on her anytime I wanted from my home office.

I wasn't such a bad mother.

Yet, I knew I was a bad mother.

13 Months Before the Breakdown

I woke to Gabriela's wails. I hurried to check on her. She was sweaty, her hair plastered to her hot little forehead.

I tried to give her some baby Tylenol, but she spit it out. I paced her room, running my hand through my hair.

By morning, she wasn't much better. She kept falling on her face. We thought she might have a bad ear infection. David took her to the doctor.

I froze when I heard the diagnosis: possible meningitis.

The doctor ordered an emergency spinal tap.

I sat outside her hospital room, rocking back and forth on the couch while talking to the doctors. I could hardly speak, I was crying so hard.

"I'll never forgive myself if something happens to her," I said.

I'd kill myself if she died.

We could bring toys to the room, but they had to be disinfected. David and I had to wear surgical masks.

As it turned out, she didn't have meningitis, which was such a relief. She had a double ear infection and a sinus infection.

The nurses cooed and tickled her feet, which caused Gabriela to giggle uncontrollably.

I watched from the doorway, wearing my mask, a good distance away.

3 Months Before the Breakdown

Our move from Mexico in fall 2004 brought another storm front. I was alone; David took Gabriela with him to a conference in Tennessee.

Pumped with caffeine, I drove 1,300 miles from Guadalajara to Santa Ana. I obsessively checked my rearview mirror for big rigs. In my luggage was Prozac that I had bought in Mexico, where I didn't need a prescription.

When I returned, at the age of 32, I was promoted to bureau editor. I was ecstatic. I'd always considered myself a leader, and here was a chance to prove myself. I demanded daily bylines from my staff, and they delivered. I routinely stayed at my desk until 10 p.m. I took work home with me and sent e-mails at 2 a.m.

By the time I got home, Gabriela was asleep, covered with her favorite pink blanket that the nanny had knitted. I worried that I was missing out. Bedtime stories, her first words, nightly baths, her sticky kisses.

When I would see her in the morning, she'd brighten and announce, "Mommy! Coffee! Mommy go work!"

I forced a smile, but I felt an ache in my chest.

3 Weeks Before the Breakdown

One afternoon at work, I received an e-mail that stopped my heart. More sexual abuse was suspected in my family in Texas. My past rose before me. I felt as if I was going to throw up. My entire body tensed, and I began to shake.

It left me unable to think, unable to sleep.

1 Week Before the Breakdown

I reached into my drawer, searching for my daily dose of Prozac. I needed it now more than ever. I realized I had missed a dose, so I doubled up. Those were my last pills.

I'd run out.

Without knowing it, I had done a very dangerous thing.

2 Days Before the Breakdown

On a routine Friday, I sat at my desk. My reporters tried to talk to me, but I wasn't listening. I apologized over and over. I felt incredibly guilty. I don't know if it was the stressful move, the new job, the horrifying e-mail, my past, the Prozac or my brain chemicals lining up wrong that day, but I fell apart. I burst into tears. Dazed and exhausted, I said I wanted to see Gabriela.

The reporters sent me home.

I called David, weeping.

"Everybody is testing me, testing me. Latino journalists are following me, watching me. I'm being filmed for a movie. They're watching me."

It was after 5 p.m., and he called a psychiatrist I hadn't seen in more than a year and a half. She wasn't there.

At home, I stared into space. *"I understand it. I finally, finally understand."*

We got under the covers that night and I whispered, *"David, are you going to lock me up in a mental hospital?"*

Sunday, Dec. 5, 2004—The Breakdown

I'm pacing, pacing.

I murdered my daughter. My little Gabriela.

The police are on their way. David strips off his bulky jacket, worried they will think he has a gun.

He's terrified that the police, thinking it is a domestic violence call, will come in with guns drawn. All the dresser drawers are pulled open and clothes are everywhere. It looks as if there has been a serious fight.

As the police rap on the door, David opens it and stares at them through the screen. At that moment a door inside slams shut with a boom.

"What was that?" the officer asks.

He walks down the hallway, checking each room, looking for Gabriela, looking for me.

He finds Gabriela first.

She's surrounded by the clothes she had thrown out of the drawers. She's happily playing with blocks.

I had never laid a hand on her, although in my mind I was sure I had.

Then the officer finds me, sitting on my bed with my head in my hands.

I instantly recognize him. Elated, I stare intensely into his eyes.

"You're my brother, my brother Jeff! Jeff? Jeff? Don't you remember me?"

She really needs to go to the emergency room, the officer tells David.

And he isn't talking about Gabriela.

He's talking about me.

• • •

Treatment briefly clears the storm clouds Video: It's Dec. 5, 2004, and I'm in the UCI emergency room. I'm trying to strip off my clothes and run down the hallway, but David restrains me.

This is a fertility experiment. David and I are brother and sister, and now they're going to separate us. I hear Gabriela crying. Where are you, my little girl? Why can't I find you?

It's Dec. 5, 2004, and I'm in the UCI emergency room. I'm trying to strip off my clothes and run down the hallway, but David restrains me.

The on-call psychiatrist walks in.

He wants to know whether I've slept. Not in three days. Whether I've been on wild spending sprees. Yes, I bought David a $450 foosball table out of the blue and gave an acquaintance $500. Talking fast? Yes. Energetic? Incredibly.

"It's bipolar disorder," he says.

I cut him off before he can say anything else.

"I killed Gabriela."

The doctor looks up from the chart.

"No she didn't," David says quickly.

But it's too late. My fate changes when I say the word "killed." I step into the world of mothers who drown their babies in bathtubs, even though I didn't do anything. The possibility is there.

Among adults bipolar disorder diagnoses have doubled in the last fifteen years.
(© Phototake, Inc./Alamy)

The security guard arrives within minutes with a wheelchair to take me across the street to the mental ward. Keys jangling from his belt, he throws a white blanket over my head to protect me from the rain. I feel like a hostage.

My heart starts to race and I'm sweating.

Inside the building, we go down a long hallway to a door with a small window. A sign reads, "AWOL risk."

I'll never see Gabriela again. I'll never see Gabriela again. I must pay for my sins.

They search through my bag to make sure I'm not carrying anything sharp. Anything I can use to slit my wrists.

I feel disoriented until it hits me.

I'm in heaven. I'm Jesus Christ.

• • •

The UCI mental ward is a sterile place, white walls, a poster extolling the virtues of electroconvulsive therapy, nurses shuffling behind glass. Blaring televisions hang from above. Security guards wearing blue gloves drag a belligerent young man away.

The nurse leads us to my room, which looks like any dorm room—two beds, a bathroom, dressers.

She tells David that if he brings me sweatpants, to make sure they're the kind without drawstrings.

Otherwise, I can use them to kill somebody.

Or myself.

How can that be? I'm already dead.

• • •

David walks down the hallway. He turns to say goodbye. Tears roll down his face.

I was right about David loving that crazy woman in the photo I saw at the University of Texas. He married her.

The door shuts.

I feel as if I can't breathe.

Later, I call him from one of the phones in the ward.

"David, please come get me. Please, please, please. I'm sorry. I won't do it again."

"Sweetie, these people are going to help you. The medicine will help you."

"This is all a big mistake. I promise I'll be good. Please, please. I need to get out of here. I need to see Gabriela."

"You need to be there. You'll see Gabriela soon."

"Don't leave me here."

"This is for your own good."

I hang up the phone and look around. Everything has blurry edges, but the center of my vision is sharp and brilliant. At a computer, a woman taps away at the keyboard.

Suddenly, a laser zaps her eyes, changing their color to an electric blue.

Confused, I run to a high-walled patio and find myself surrounded by slow-moving, wide-eyed, drugged people. They seem to float, swirling through the cloudy cigarette smoke.

I back away from them.

I run inside and find the ward empty, lights dimmed. Near the phones stands a man wearing shorts. I approach him and look searchingly into his oval face.

Oh, my God. It's my ex-boyfriend's brother. That woman at the computer is his sister. The whole family is here. They've trapped me in this place. Now I'll never, ever get to see David.

The man leans toward me, as if to share a secret. He mumbles something and then offers a slight smile. *I don't understand. I don't understand.*

He mumbles again. And again. And again.

Until it starts to sound as if he is saying, "It's all right. It's all right. It's all right."

• • •

The next day, a nurse approaches, carrying a tray of white cups. I clamp my mouth shut, shaking my head no.

They're poisoning me.

They label me a 5150, which means I am a danger to myself or others, that I am there involuntarily. That lays the legal groundwork to force me to take my meds and keeps me a prisoner for at least 72 hours.

I am officially crazy.

Gabriela is at home, safe. I'm in jail, where I belong.

Suddenly, the whole thing strikes me as hilarious, and I can't stop laughing.

I used to make fun of 5150s as a cops reporter. Crazy, naked women who led police on foot chases. Insane men who broke down in public, crying hysterically. People who didn't take their medication. People who ended up in mental wards for good.

• • •

The nurses won't let Gabriela visit. I'm too unpredictable, too scary to see my daughter. *The television sends me messages. They're poisoning me with the food. All of us in the ward are dead.*

When David arrives, I snap back to reality when he mentions Gabriela.

"So how is she?" I ask him. "Does she ask for me?"

"She does ask about you. She misses you very much."

That makes me smile.

David does what the nurses couldn't do: He persuades me to take my medication.

I place my hand on David's knee. Barbara, a middle-aged patient with short-cropped hair, taps me on the shoulder.

"There is no touching allowed here."

"He's my husband."

"It doesn't matter. There is no touching allowed here."

"He's my husband."

"I will deal with you later," Barbara says.

She flips me off and walks away. I follow her with my eyes.

Feisty. I like that.

She's somebody I can be friends with.

• • •

Barbara wears mascara and red lipstick. She loves to sing Rod Stewart songs, snapping her fingers and bobbing her head while belting out "Maggie May." When she speaks, her eyes grow wide, her hands wave wildly. She has a very foul mouth.

I think she's beautiful.

I follow her around, seeking advice and comfort. Using my CD player, we sing and dance to Dolly Parton tunes in the visiting room, prancing over the sunbeams on the floor.

I sit next to her one day, in a delusional but good mood.

"I want to be a missionary, a missionary in Mexico."

She smiles beatifically.

Barbara tells me that all sorts of people can be missionaries, even crazy people.

That strikes me as the wisest thing I've ever heard.

It gives me hope.

• • •

By my third day, I become the object of affection of two men who follow me around the ward, smiling suggestively. One is the man who keeps saying, "It's all right. It's all right." The other is a short man who is an expert ping-pong player.

I know I must be getting better when I sit next to my admirer and challenge him to a game. I really, really want to play. I absolutely must play.

I have a burning desire to win. The old Val is coming back.

• • •

On the eighth day, I sit in the sunny, white room with the on-call doctor. We are chatting, when my "all right" admirer shows up. He stands way too close to me, our knees practically touching.

"Man, he really does like you," the doctor says.

She and I look at each other and burst out laughing.

"You've got that right."

I suddenly realize that I have crossed the line.

The doctor and I are one side. The crazy people are on the other.

I look around the room. Barbara dances alone. Another man wanders aimlessly, talking to himself. My "all right" admirer hisses at me not to trust the doctor.

I feel sorry for them and wonder if they'll ever leave this place.

I'm incredibly lucky because I know that I will.

The doctors have decided that I've steadily improved and am ready to go home. It all seems so sudden to me, and I have to pack immediately.

I can't believe it. I finally get to see Gabriela.

• • •

When I walk into the house, I scoop up a beaming Gabriela and kiss her cheeks. I run my hands through her soft curls. I squeeze her little pudgy toes.

Even though I'm happy to be home, something isn't right. It's Christmastime. But I can't quite get into the spirit. I'm pale and sickly.

I sit on the couch, surrounded by the Christmas tree and Nativity scene that David put up, and stare into space for hours. On the weekends, I sleep for 20 hours a day. Gabriela runs into the room. "Mommy, Mommy, wake up!" I bury myself under the covers. David, terrified of what I might do to myself, checks on me every half hour, making sure I'm still alive.

One day in the kitchen, I pick up a gleaming knife and hold it to my wrist. Just to see what it feels like. I imagine carving my pale skin like a piece of wood, crimson rising to the surface. I throw the knife in the sink and go to my dresser in search of my pills.

I hold the bottle of sleeping pills. I grip it. I want to take them. What if I took them all?

A smiling Gabriela suddenly appears at my side.

"Mommy? Mommy take medicine?"

I put the bottle away.

In February 2005, I confess to my psychiatrist that I'm suicidal. He realizes the medications aren't working. He places me in St. Joseph Hospital's mental ward. The doctors try different doses and different drugs, they try different combinations. We are running out of options.

Except for one. A terrifying one. Something I've only seen in the movies.

Will extreme measures work where normal ones haven't?

The doctor didn't say the word, but I heard it. Very clearly.

Electroshock.

My heart skipped. Do they still do that?

The doctor is going on about "electroconvulsive therapy," but my mind is spinning.

Two cables, like the kind used to jump cars, are attached to my head. My face contorts. My body flails. My head is on fire. I smell burning hair. I'm stupid. I'm drooling.

Hell, no.

But David feels differently.

"The medication isn't working," he says.

"I rely on my brain. I'm a reporter."

"I'm worried you're going to kill yourself," David says.

I'm worried it's going to kill my memory.

After several conversations throughout February, we agreed to the treatment that would have the least impact. They would zap only one side of my brain.

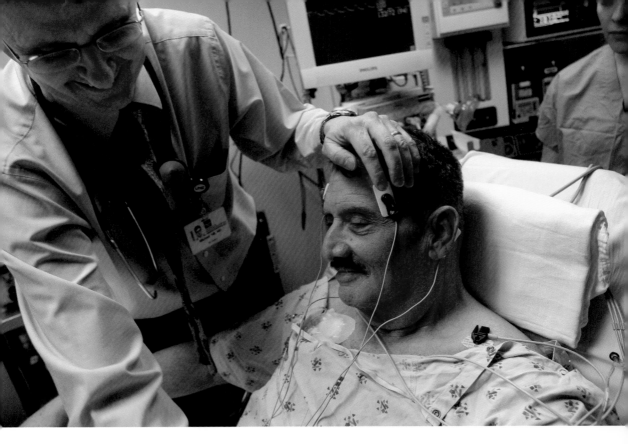

As part of treatment for bipolar depression some patients go through the rigors of electroshock therapy. The treatment is controversial. (Ethan Hyman/MCT/Landov)

When I think about it now, I know the real reason I agreed was Gabriela.

A mother undergoing electro-shock is better than a mother who commits suicide.

It's noon, but my room at St. Joseph is dark and the curtains are closed. I'm lying on my side, staring at the wall. In the other bed is a pretty librarian who is in the hospital because she slit her wrists.

I'm about to drift off again, when Dr. Himasiri De Silva appears at my bedside. He gets the tough cases at St. Joseph.

He smiles warmly and introduces himself. I instantly like Dr. De Silva. He has the kindest eyes and focuses on just me. His beeper goes off, but he ignores it. He's the kind of doctor, I later learn, who calls you back within an hour. And he's been a psychiatrist for more than 30 years.

Well, I figure, if I'm going to do ECT, I'm going to do it with him.

• • •

During my four-day stay at St. Joseph, I track down patients who had ECT.

One middle-age man swears by it, but he looks dazed, almost zombie-like.

Then there's the young engineer. The one with a degree from UC Berkeley.

I press him for details.

"What was it like?"

He shrugs, smiles and then looks away.

"I forgot how to do my multiplication tables."

Oh, my God.

• • •

It's Feb. 25, 2005. It's 5:30 a.m. I'm wearing sweatpants and my Curious George T-shirt. I'm in the ward, filling out a depression survey that, frankly, depresses me. Every answer reveals that I'm in worse shape than I thought.

A sweet nurse takes me in a wheelchair to a room filled with hospital equipment that reminds me of the day Gabriela was born. The happiest day of my life seems far away.

I scoot up on the gurney. A blood-pressure cuff hangs over the rail. Next to me is a blue box a little bigger than a VCR. That's where the electricity comes from.

I stare at the ceiling. I want to cry, but I have no tears. I sigh heavily. I'm not nervous, just resigned. I feel glued to the gurney.

The nurses murmur encouragingly and hook me up with leads—head, chest, left leg—to monitor my heart, brain and muscle activity.

I feel helpless, as if something has been set in motion that I can't undo. But I also feel as if I'm among people who care about me. People who understand depression. A nurse lovingly tucks a warm blanket around my legs.

The anesthesiologist wraps my arm with a rubber tube and tightens it to get the IV needle in. He's handsome, and I suddenly feel self-conscious about my greasy hair. The needle goes into the IV tube, injecting propofol, an anesthetic. In less than a minute, I'm asleep.

• • •

To find out for this story what happens during the rest of the procedure, I go back to St. Joseph a year later to observe an ECT. I think it will be easy to handle. It isn't.

When I see the gurney, my heart starts to pound. I've been here. In this very spot. I feel lightheaded.

After they put you to sleep, the doctor administers succinylcholine, a muscle relaxant that paralyzes you and makes your calf ripple.

I feel nauseated watching it.

You can't breathe on your own, so they place the Air-Shields Manual Breathing Unit over your face. The blue bag breathes for you.

Dr. De Silva slides on his rubber gloves. He squeezes gel onto the electrode pads and places them on your head. The nurse holds your arms so they don't bang against the rail during the convulsion. Then they put in the brown mouth guard so you don't bite your tongue.

Dr. De Silva walks to the box, flicks on the green power switch. The electricity shoots through your brain for eight seconds. There is no spasm, no noise, at this point.

It's when the electricity stops that the brain triggers a convulsion.

You grimace. Your legs curl into a fetal position and your body stiffens. After about 40 seconds, you go limp.

I'm watching, holding my breath, clenching my notebook. My heart races.

I feel drained, as if I might fall over. The doctor monitors the machine, which spits out a brainwave report.

I want to speak, but I can't. No words form in my brain. I just stand there, staring at the patient, who lies motionless.

•••

I remember what it's like to wake up. While I'm on the gurney, I groggily open my eyes. I look around and smile.

A nurse stops by to chat.

"Would you like a cup of coffee?"

•••

They're not sure how electro-shock works. When my brain is shocked, it triggers a seizure. During my seizure, neurotransmitters, mood-related chemicals, are released, but they're not sure how many. Unlike Prozac, which targets serotonin, ECT doesn't target specific neurotransmitters.

It has an 80 percent success rate, and my doctors say I've improved. Maybe I have, but I feel like part of the 20 percent.

ECT also does a tremendous job of destroying memory. I lost memory from a year before the treatment to several months after it.

•••

When you get ECT, they make you sign a contract saying you won't drive a car during the course of your treatment. But a month after my first treatment, I couldn't stick to that rule.

"I'm going to the gym," I tell David.

"You know you're not supposed to drive," he replies.

But in a rare moment, I suddenly need to get out of the house, which has been my tomb for months.

I get into our gray Volkswagen. The route to the gym should be easy. I've taken it many times. It's a straight shot down the freeway, less than three miles away.

But I never even make it to the freeway. I don't even make it out of our neighborhood. I start to sweat. I turn the air conditioning up high. My hands are shaking. I don't have my cell phone.

I spend two hours driving up and down Bristol Street, completely lost.

I pass KFC again. It hits me. That's the KFC on the corner where I turn to go home. I'm saved by fried chicken. My breathing steadies as I drive past familiar houses. I pull up to our house and walk in.

"Where have you been? You had me so worried," David says.

I feel so ashamed. I put away the car keys.

I don't say a word.

• • •

The air conditioner in our bedroom window hums loudly. It's hot outside on this June evening. David and I are getting ready for bed.

"You know," David says, "we need a romantic getaway."

"I agree," I say absent-mindedly. I'm engrossed in a book about bipolar disorder.

"Something like Catalina. Like we did on Valentine's Day," he says.

"Catalina? What the hell are you talking about?"

"You don't remember Catalina? We went there the whole weekend. I rented us a beautiful room with an ocean view."

I'm stunned. I have absolutely no recollection of our trip. I put down my book.

I quiz him. What else happened this spring? A neighbor's party. Don't remember it. The friends who brought me food. Don't remember a single one. The work party celebrating our team being finalists for a Pulitzer. It's as if it never happened.

I feel my face grow hot. I panic. How did I act at these events? Did I babble? Act crazy? Did I talk about the sexual abuse?

A co-worker at the Pulitzer party later tells me it sounded as if I was on painkillers. I wore a goofy smile all night.

Typically, patients get 10 to 12 ECT treatments. I had 14.

I later find out that all sorts of big things happened around the time I was getting treatments. Johnnie Cochran died. "Deep Throat" was revealed. The pope died.

The world passed me by.

• • •

I'm not getting any better. If anything, my depression is getting worse.

One Saturday, I'm sitting on the couch. David is going to take Gabriela to the park.

"Mommy, come with us."

I stare right through her.

David picks her up and walks out the door.

She looks at me over David's shoulder, gives me a big smile and waves goodbye.

I feel my heart break.

• • •

It's June 2005. I end up at St. Joseph. Suicidal. Again.

By now, I absolutely hate hospitals. Time goes slower in the hospital. The televisions always have bad reception. The air is stale. They don't let you have coffee with caffeine in it. Can you believe that?

One day, I notice a woman standing near the phones.

"Why are you here?" I ask.

"I found my daughter dead, hanging."

I gasp. "I'm so, so sorry."

She puts her hands in her pockets and sadly looks away.

"Yeah, she was my bud."

If I needed evidence of the impact of suicide, there it was. I couldn't do that to my family, not to Gabriela.

I beg Dr. De Silva to let me out. He says he will, on one condition—that I try "partial hospitalization," a group-therapy program. Fine. Anything to get me out of here.

I hope this program works, because my disease is starting to manifest itself in different ways. In very ugly ways.

Therapy explores mind's dark places

A serial killer lurks in the house.

I dive into the closets, looking for him behind the clothes. I count the knives to make sure he hasn't taken any. I check under the beds. Then I look in the closets again. And then again.

My husband, David Fitzgerald, is about to leave the house to go to the gym one day in June 2005, and I freeze. I can't be alone.

I should know no one is there. I should know the serial killer is in my head. He is my grandfather stalking me. But in my mind, I see the killer slit my throat, I fall to the floor, watching him move toward Gabriela.

I can't save my daughter.

I know my house is safe. Lots of stay-at-home moms live in the neighborhood, where their kids play in the street. One of my neighbors is a police officer who keeps a close eye on things.

But it gets to be so bad, we have to fly family members in to stay with me while David goes on out-of-town job interviews.

I try hard not to let Gabriela see me frightened. When she sees me looking in the closets, I pretend I'm looking for a scarf. I don't want to alarm her. I'm sitting on the bed one day and she comes up to me. She holds my face, looks into my eyes and asks, "Mommy, are you scared?"

"No," I lie.

• • •

Clearly, ECT didn't make me sane. My psychiatrist, Dr. Himasiri De Silva, thinks that the treatments helped. David does, too. I'm not so sure. I lost too much memory. But I don't regret doing it. It wasn't a procedure that I rushed into. I had a second opinion, as state law requires. I was so depressed that I would have tried anything.

And I know it saves lives. I've seen it save the lives of other patients.

PERSPECTIVES ON DISEASES AND DISORDERS

But to be honest, I wouldn't do it again. I'd rather just rely on medication.

• • •

I come out of the bathroom, worried and pale.

"David, I think I have colon cancer."

"You don't have cancer."

I set up a doctor's appointment anyway.

It's not the only one I make. I get a backache. *Leukemia.* I have an abnormal pap smear (which later comes back fine). *Cervical cancer.* My breasts feel sore one week. *Breast cancer.* And what's wrong with my *lymph nodes*?

I'm dying. I just know it.

I spend hours on the Internet, researching not my mental illness but all the other diseases I imagine I have. Gabriela appears at my side, stuffed animals in hand, ready to have a tea party.

"Five minutes," I tell her and get back to my "research."

She stamps her foot, with hands on her hips, and screams, "No! No five minutes!"

I stop typing and look at her. Is it the terrible twos? Or have I passed this horrible thing on to her? After all, it's believed to be genetic. Statistics show that Gabriela has a 15 percent to 30 percent chance of having bipolar disorder.

Gabriela stops screaming and looks up at me, tears in her eyes. My head suddenly hurts.

Oh, no. A brain tumor.

• • •

One day, I'm in particularly bad shape. The depression makes my limbs so heavy that I can barely walk. I drop to the floor and crawl to the bathroom from my bed, where I have been all day. David calls Dr. De Silva for advice.

Dr. De Silva tells him that it takes time for the medication to work. He's added lithium to the mix. We need to be patient.

"I guarantee you 100 percent that she will get better," he tells David.

When I hear that, I feel relieved. Somewhere inside me, I believe him.

So, when Dr. De Silva suggests group therapy, I don't hesitate.

I trust him.

. . .

I'm wearing a new blouse that I bought at a plus-size women's store, and it humiliates me. I've gained 40 pounds. It's partly the medication, but it's partly because I know the guys at In-N-Out Burger by name.

I'm in "partial hospitalization," group therapy, at St. Joseph Hospital, where I will go for six hours every weekday for three months. I'm sitting with an account executive, a dentist, a college professor, a company vice president and a stay-at-home mom. We sit at a brown conference table in a bland room with two leather couches in the corner.

A poster listing famous people who suffered from mental illness hangs on the wall. Ernest Hemingway and Sylvia Plath are on the list. It's meant to show how successful you can be, but all I can think is that they killed themselves. Sunlight spills across half the table, thanks to a giant skylight. By the afternoon, the direct sunlight is unbearable, and we move to the other side.

I try to hide my hands, which are trembling because of the lithium.

The group leader, a licensed counselor with a soft voice, asks me to introduce myself.

I love the look on their faces when I proudly tell them I had electroshock therapy. I brag about being a 5150. I show off when I tell them I thought I was Jesus Christ. I am a badass. I am special. I know I am going to floor them.

Until a young woman pipes up, "Hey, I thought I was the messiah, too. You and I sound exactly alike."

So, I'm not special. These people have gone through what I've gone through. We're much more alike than I realized.

I'm the one who is floored.

During break, I stare at the crude drawings on the wall. Many are in crayon with inspirational phrases such as "You can do it!" and "I love myself."

Cheesy, I think.

But truth is, I'm jealous. Because the people who drew those pictures have finished the program, and that means they're better. I am so far away from that place that I can't even imagine it. All I can do is stare at their work.

• • •

Depression erases the days, the months. The best thing about group therapy, I later realize, is that it gives me somewhere to go every day. It forces me to get out of bed and be somewhere on time.

The day, supervised by a licensed counselor, starts out with goals, short-term and long-term. Mine are always the same: eat healthy and exercise and return to work.

Then we get a sheet with a silhouette of a man. The questions include, "What do you like about this person? What don't you like?"

A box of crayons, markers and colored pencils sits in the middle of the table. I go for the crayons and draw as best as I can with my shaky hand the face of one of the men who molested me. I use the colors black and red to represent his nasty temper.

I think about the questions before answering them. I like that he always seemed interested in my life. He attended my sporting events. Sometimes, we played basketball on weekends and went running together.

I don't like that he sexually abused me. But he has apologized, and I've forgiven him. I've made peace with the situation. But I'll never leave Gabriela alone with him.

This is art therapy.

After we're done, I feel like a third-grader. My hand shoots into the air. Pick me! Pick me! I can't wait to explain my drawing.

• • •

After break, we come back to find two empty chairs facing each other. We're going to do role-playing. You sit in the chair and have a pretend conversation with the person you're having problems with. Then you imagine how the other person would respond.

A man sits up at the front, engaged in an imaginary conversation with his mother.

But my mind starts to wander, and I imagine myself up there in the chair.

I picture myself talking to Gabriela. Lately, I let her eat whatever she wants. I let her stay up late and watch videos nonstop. I do anything she demands to avoid a temper tantrum. I feel guilty saying no to her because I've been so emotionally distant.

I'm sitting in the chair, playing my part and Gabriela's part, too.

"No, Gabriela, you cannot have cookies for dinner. You can have a cookie, one cookie, after dinner."

"No, mommy! I want cookies. Give me cookies."

"I know you want cookies, but you can't have any until after dinner. That's the rule."

I imagine that she begins to scream.

I pluck her from the chair and give her a timeout.

She shrieks.

I imagine that I hold her arms to keep her in her timeout. I count out loud. We reach two minutes.

She starts to calm down.

I let her out of timeout, and we have dinner.

The exercise teaches me that I can discipline my child lovingly, responsibly. I shouldn't be afraid to set boundaries for her. She needs boundaries. She wants boundaries.

• • •

At first, when I joined group therapy, I thought everybody was, well, crazy. One woman heard voices screaming in her head. Another was a "cutter" who had dozens of red scars on her arms. Several people in the group had tried to kill themselves, one by stabbing herself in the stomach.

I never thought I'd become friends with these people, but that's exactly what happens. I get to know three very smart women.

We meet at Olive Garden for three-hour lunches. We share our setbacks and our successes, cheering each other on. We complain about the side effects of our medication—the weight gain, the acne, the shakes. It's like a free therapy session.

One tried to kill herself with pills. Another suffers from terrifying panic attacks. Another, severe depression. And then there is me, the bipolar person.

We are the faces of mental illness.

Bipolar and Going to College

Lynette Clemetson

In the following article Lynette Clemetson writes about the challenges facing two young adults with bipolar disorder as they transition from high school to college. Jean Lynch-Thomason and Chris Ference were both diagnosed with bipolar disorder as children and have lived with the disorder for several years. They each approach moving away from the support and structure of their homes, families, and therapists in different ways. Jean is confident and ready to attend college, which in her case happens to be thousands of miles from home. Jean's parents, however, are anxious about the move. Chris, on the other hand, initially wanted to live at home and attend a nearby college. It was his parents' encouragement that motivated him to attend a college farther away and live on campus. According to Clemetson, students with mental illnesses, like Jean and Chris, are becoming more common on college campuses. Clemetson has written for *Newsweek* and *The New York Times*.

Her mother called it a negotiable proposition. But to Jean Lynch-Thomason, a 17-year-old with bipolar disorder who started college this fall [2006], her mom's notion to fly from their home in Nashville to her campus in Olympia, Wash., every few weeks to monitor Jean's illness felt needlessly intrusive.

"I am so totally aware of the control you have over me right now," Jean said, sitting in her parents' living room one evening last June, before coolly reminding her mother of her upcoming 18th birthday. "In a few months the power dynamic is going to be different."

For Chris Ference, 19, who is also bipolar, the fast-approaching autonomy of his freshman year held somewhat less appeal. His parents had always directed every aspect of his mental health care. Last summer, over Friday night pizza at his home in Cranberry Township, Pa., he told them that assuming control felt more daunting than liberating.

"If it was up to me, I would just have it so you could make those decisions for me up until I was like, 22," he said. "I mean, you've raised me well up to now. You know me better than anyone."

Transitioning from High School to College Can Be Tricky for Anyone

The transition from high school to college, from adolescence to legal adulthood, can be tricky for any teenager, but for the increasing number of young people who arrive on campus with diagnoses of serious mental disorders—and for their parents—the passage can be particularly fraught.

Standard struggles with class schedules, roommates, and sexual and social freedom are complicated by decisions about if or when to use campus counseling services, whether or not to take medication and whether to disclose an illness to friends or professors.

Keeping a psychiatric disorder under control in an environment often fueled by all-night cram sessions, junk food and heavy drinking is a challenge for even the most motivated students. In addition, the normal separation that goes along with college requires new roles and boundaries with parents, the people who best know the history and contours of their illness.

Like Jean and Chris, young adults approach the move to a new life differently, some with defiant independence, some with avoidance. Each approach, say psychiatrists, counselors, dormitory assistants and other campus leaders, comes with its own risk. The students who are most dependent on their parents may be dangerously unprepared for the inevitable stresses of college life. On the other hand, students who are adamant about doing everything on their own may be afraid to reach out for help when they stumble.

For parents, the anxious pride at seeing children go off to college is often tinged with fear that their child might fall apart, spiraling into depression or becoming suicidal. Are they going to therapy as they promised? Are they taking the right dose of medication at the right time? Should they as parents inform the school that their child has an illness? Is a fight with a roommate part of a normal transition to college life or a sign of impending trouble? Does an emotional e-mail message written at 3 A.M. represent a transitory moment of turmoil or a reason to get on an airplane?

Once teenagers legally become adults, which in most states happens at age 18, they, not their parents, assume control over decisions about therapy and medication. If trouble arises, parents may or may not hear about it because college counselors are bound by confidentiality when dealing with adult students.

Jean Is Ready for Autonomy

For Jean, as for many teenagers coping with mental disorders, just getting through high school was an ordeal. After experimenting with home schooling, a high pressure prep school and an outdoor learning academy geared to nature activities, Jean, a bright student with inconsistent grades but high SAT [Scholastic Aptitude Test] scores, decided to forgo her senior year and find a college that would take her without a high school diploma.

She was accepted at Evergreen State College in Olympia, Wash., a nontraditional college of roughly 4,400 students that issues written evaluations in place of letter grades.

Evergreen's environmental focus—the campus has its own organic farm, composting program and a contest for commuters who bike, walk or carpool to campus—felt like a good fit for Jean, who is passionately committed to the environment and social justice.

A consciously quirky teenager who sews her own clothes (to avoid crass consumerism, she says) and who prefers bus trips to flying (to avoid contributing to the pollution caused by air travel), Jean is disarmingly straightforward and self-aware.

She said she stopped taking medications when she was 14 because the side effects left her feeling "out of whack and emotionally inauthentic."

She is determined to stay off medications during college, and she devoted considerable advance thought to possible triggers for her illness, like the long rainy winters of the Pacific Northwest.

"I don't feel vulnerable about this transition because this is very much my decision," she said. "This is a very autonomous move, very much me structuring my own life. I feel like I am putting myself in a situation with really clear intentions."

Jean's parents, Amy Lynch, 52, and Phil Thomason, 53, were hesitant when Jean, the younger of their two daughters, refused to take medications after eighth grade. Her childhood and early adolescence had been a whirlwind of depression, rage and experiments with different medications and treatments.

But when Jean was about 14, Ms. Lynch and Mr. Thomason said, she began to seem more stable. Her developing coping skills, combined with reports about negative side effects of psychotropic drugs in children, persuaded them to acquiesce to her demands to ride out the swings of her illness drug free.

They said they believed Evergreen would be a good college for Jean. Still, the move—to someplace so far from home—made them anxious. In the months before Jean left, Ms. Lynch said she wanted her to go back on medication to smooth the adjustment to college life, a suggestion that Jean adamantly rejected.

Ms. Lynch worried that Jean took for granted the tacit stability of being at home. When Jean's depression sets in, she tends to close herself off from people. At home, Ms. Lynch said, "I can look at Jean and know in five minutes what's going on with her and how to respond to it."

At such a distance it will be difficult to catch the signs. "I feel like we're doing a high-wire act," she said, "and I am not sure we have a strong enough net."

Rummaging through the accumulated possessions of adolescence in her bedroom over the summer, Jean singled out the items that she could not leave without: her sewing machine, her coffee maker, the social justice posters that covered her wall.

With her mother out of earshot, she acknowledged that she understood her parents' angst. "I get that this is intense for everyone," she said. "I do."

Chris Is Reluctant to Leave the Nest

The uncertain months between high school and college were also anxious ones for Chris Ference and his parents.

Still groggy from an early morning drive to campus, his husky 6-foot-2 frame jammed into an auditorium chair in the student union, Chris shifted uncomfortably as a freshman orientation coordinator welcomed new students and their parents to the Behrend College, a Pennsylvania State University satellite campus in Erie, Pa.

"Today really is the first day of your freshman year of college," the cheery administrator told the group on a June morning more than two months before the start of fall term.

Chris had initially been reluctant to go away to college. Though eager to leave the rigid structure and peer pressure of high school, where he told few friends about his illness, he preferred the idea of living at home during college and commuting to an engineering program in nearby Pittsburgh.

It was his mother, Debbie Ference, a service director with the southwestern Pennsylvania division of the National Alliance on Mental Illness, an advocacy group, who nudged him to move away.

He chose Behrend for its strong engineering program and small student body of about 3,700.

A boyish and fidgety teenager who likes heavy metal music, Xbox games and anything having to do with electronics, Chris said he had given little advance thought to his new responsibilities in college.

Just days before his orientation, he listened passively as his father, Michael Ference, and Ms. Ference talked about his care at school. They wondered aloud about whether he would be able to continue seeing his longtime therapist in Pittsburgh, more than two hours away. They raised the possibility of putting an advance mental health directive in place, so that they could be contacted if Chris was ever in crisis and unable to consent to parental notification.

They discussed how they worried about the possibility of Chris mixing alcohol with his medications. Chris huffed in annoyance and told them he was "smart and moral enough" not to fall into that trap.

The fact that Chris was willing to engage in the discussion at all was a sign, they said, of progress.

Chris was first hospitalized and received a diagnosis of bipolar disorder at age 10 after a severe episode of depression, mania and suicidal thoughts. He was hospitalized again briefly in sixth grade, after the lithium that had stabilized him for two years became ineffective.

But successful therapy and medication since then have kept the illness at a manageable level. He graduated from high school with honors, and in his senior year saw his therapist only every six weeks. A recent medication adjustment has left him able to feel and express more than he has in years.

"This whole move is like a coming-out process," said Mr. Ference, 50, a service coordinator for families with autistic children. "Up to now it's been all parental motivation. But I think this is a healing process for him after so many hard years."

More and More College Students Are on Psychiatric Meds

In a 2005 national survey of the directors of college counseling centers, 95 percent of counseling directors reported an increase in students who were already on psychiatric medications when they came in for help. While universities grapple with how to serve the growing number of students with mental disorders, students are taking the initiative by helping one another.

Active Minds, a student-led mental health advocacy organization founded in 2001 at the University of Pennsylvania, now [2006] has 56 chapters at schools including Georgetown University, Columbia University, the University of South Florida and the University of Maryland.

The National Alliance on Mental Illness has 30 campus affiliates, with 18 more in formation, groups that are set up as student clubs and are financed by school activity budgets and fund-raisers. Programs like the Jed Foundation, a suicide prevention program, and National Depression Screening Day, held each October, offer additional resources.

While the overall message from the groups and programs focuses on the potential for success, students who

Students with mental illnesses living on college campuses is much more common today than in the past. (© David R. Frazier Photolibrary, Inc./Alamy)

have been through the transition of leaving home for college say it is also important to be honest about the challenges. . . .

Last-Minute Worries

After the opening session of freshman orientation at Behrend College back in June [2006], Chris Ference disappeared into a pack of students to begin selecting his classes.

His mother headed in the opposite direction and wandered into a session on student support networks led by Sue Daley, the director of the counseling office. She listened intently as the counselor talked about problems students had encountered in recent years.

She winced when the counselor related the story of a young woman who had a psychotic episode the previous year, during which she ripped tiles from her dormitory room ceiling because she believed the F.B.I. was moni-

PERSPECTIVES ON DISEASES AND DISORDERS

toring her. "We sent her home so she could get her emotional self together," Ms. Daley told the group.

After the session, Ms. Ference complained that it sounded as if the goal of the counseling center was to get the "crazy kids" out of the way. "I was offended by that," she said to Ms. Daley. "I want to be comfortable enough with this school that I know you will take care of my son."

In the car on the way home from the campus visit, Ms. Ference mentioned her discomfort with the counseling presentation. "We definitely have to put some outside counseling support in place, just in case you don't like it there," she said to her son.

Looking through his thick pamphlet of brochures from the day, Chris responded, "Hey, we get a discount on computers and iPods!"

Ms. Ference took a hand off the steering wheel to rub at the stress headache pulsating at her temple.

More Fear than Letting On

About the same time in June at Bongo Java, a trendy coffee shop near her home in the Belmont-Hillsboro section of Nashville, Jean Lynch-Thomason pulled out a tattered journal, held together with silver duct tape. A picture of herself in the third grade, taped to the cover of the thick diary, stared back at her as she gathered her thoughts.

As she prepared for college, she had been writing in the journal several times a day. More pensive than during the previous meeting when she matched wits with her parents about her desired independence, Jean confessed that she had been thinking quite a lot about her move in the fall.

"There is a lot more fear and anxiety about this transition than I am letting on," she said. "We can set up all the protective measures we want and still there is just no way to tell what is going to happen, and man, that's hard."

She remained determined not to let her mother fly out to Washington to check on her. And she resolved to limit her own trips home, to cut down on unnecessary air travel.

But she said she felt confident that she had done the most optimal planning possible. She had decided to have an apartment by herself so that she could prepare her own vegan meals. Living alone, she said, would also afford her the privacy to sleep well and have the solitude she craves when her depression sets in. That solitude, she added, might be a double-edged sword in a new environment where she would be more reluctant to engage with people during dark periods of depression.

"I am in a good, copacetic place right now," she said. "But I also know that there is every possibility that things could go bad. I just sort of feel like if I get out there and don't do well, then I am letting everyone down."

Back at home soon after, she breezed past her mother, confident as ever.

A New Perspective

Three months after arriving on campus, Jean's anger at her parents' concern seems to have receded. Her mother's hotly debated first visit came and went in October. There were no confrontations over medication, no accusations of heavy-handedness.

Mother and daughter said little at all, in fact, about the illness that has so defined their lives, and their relationship, choosing instead to ride bikes, work at a free store for the needy, and play in a fountain one night in the center of downtown.

"I'm more settled, I guess," said Jean, who will turn 18 next week [December 2006]. She was surprised that she so enjoyed the visit. "I was in a good place. She was in a good place. My illness just didn't particularly seem relevant."

Some ideas that had made sense in the abstract—like living alone—felt unwise after she arrived in September and looked at a few apartments. When a friend from Tennessee offered her a tiny crawl space of a room in an overcrowded home he shared with several other students off campus, Jean said it felt just right.

"It's not like I'm going up to people saying, 'Hi, I'm Jean, I'm bipolar,' " she joked. "But I'm surrounded by beautiful supportive people, and I know if I need it, they will call me out."

She has maintained sessions by telephone with her therapist back home every two weeks. But she has also met people at the campus counseling center. She said she liked that they encouraged holistic as well as purely medical approaches to treatment, and that she would not hesitate to seek help there if the need arose.

Back in Nashville, Ms. Lynch said she may have underestimated her daughter's ability to make good decisions for herself. The lushness and environmental consciousness of Evergreen and the surrounding area seemed to have a stabilizing effect on Jean, she said. There was not a trace of the early signs of mania or depression that Ms. Lynch could usually spot in her daughter well before others.

She said she had decided not to raise the issue of medication again. For now. "I may have a different answer a few months from now," she said. "But what I know today is that she seems to have learned a lot about coping. And that's how we get through this, by what we know any given day."

"Things Are Just Going So Good"

Chris Ference has also changed since he packed his things and left home in late August [2006]. Sitting on the bed in his dorm room, sounding more mature than he had a few months earlier, he said the transition was smoother than he had anticipated.

But he was still working out some of the particulars of dealing with his bipolar disorder. He told his roommate

FAST FACT

One in three college students reports having experienced prolonged periods of depression, according to a National Alliance on Mental Illness survey.

about his illness in mid-October, only because a reporter was coming to their room for an interview.

"It's cool. He's cool. It's fine," he said, with a hint of wariness. "It's probably good for him to know anyway, so he can understand it, in case I ever need him to help me out."

Discreetly taking his medications in a dorm room typically crammed with engineering students until the wee hours of the morning is also a challenge. In an effort not to draw attention to himself, he said, he takes his two medications late at night, right before he lays his head down to sleep. If anyone notices, they have not let on.

He and his mother met with Ms. Daley, head of the counseling center, before school started. After the unpleasant encounter at summer orientation, Ms. Ference wanted some assurances that the school's services were adequate. She left satisfied, she said, and Chris seemed comfortable enough with the counseling center to go there if he needed to.

Chris said he doubted he would need help from Ms. Daley or anyone else at the center. He has friends and is playing guitar in a band, he keeps his partying "under control," and he loves his engineering classes.

He is under no illusions about his illness, he said. He knows it will be something that he has to learn to manage throughout his adult life.

"But things are just going so good," he said. "So far."

GLOSSARY

amygdala An almond-shaped structure in the temporal lobe of the brain and a part of the limbic system. It is involved in the processing of emotions and memories and is implicated in many psychiatric disorders.

anhedonia A condition characterized by loss of the capacity to experience pleasure or the inability to gain pleasure from acts that normally produce it; a feature of major depression.

anticonvulsant Medication used to control or prevent seizures and also used to treat bipolar disorder. Drug groups include benzodiazepines and barbiturates.

antidepressant A medication used to treat depression. Drug groups known as SSRIs, MAOIs, and tricyclics are particularly associated with the term.

antipsychotic Medication used to alleviate psychoses, such as schizophrenia. Examples are haloperidol, a "typical antipsychotic," and risperidone, an "atypical antipsychotic."

bipolar disorder A depressive disorder in which a person alternates between episodes of major depression and mania.

bipolar I Known as "raging bipolar." Characterized by at least one full-blown manic episode lasting at least one week, or any duration if hospitalization is required. This may include inflated self-esteem or grandiosity, decreased need for sleep, distractibility, and excessive involvement in risky activities.

bipolar II Known as "swinging bipolar." Characterized by at least one major depressive episode plus at least one hypomanic episode over at least four days. No psychotic features.

clinical trials | Trials to evaluate the effectiveness and safety of medications or medical devices by monitoring their effects on large groups of people.

cyclothymia | Characterized by symptoms (but not necessarily full episodes of) hypomania and mild depression. One-third of those with cyclothymia are eventually diagnosed as bipolar.

delusion | Strongly held false belief that causes a person to misinterpret events and relationships.

Depakote | *See* valproic acid

depression | A mood disorder characterized by a range of symptoms that may include feeling depressed most of the time, loss of pleasure, feelings of worthlessness, and suicidal thoughts, as well as physical states that may affect eating and sleeping and other activities.

depressive disorders | A group of diseases, including major depressive disorder (commonly referred to as major depression), dysthymia, bipolar disorder (manic depression), postpartum depression, and seasonal affective disorder.

Diagnostic and Statistical Manual of Mental Disorders, 4th Edition (DSM-IV) | A book published by the American Psychiatric Association that gives general descriptions and characteristic symptoms of different mental illnesses. Physicians and other mental health professionals use the *DSM-IV* to confirm diagnoses for mental illnesses.

dopamine | A neurotransmitter known to have multiple functions depending on where it acts. Dopamine is thought to regulate emotional responses and play a role in schizophrenia and cocaine abuse.

dysthymia | A type of depressive disorder that is less severe than major depressive disorder but is more persistent. The *DSM-IV* mandates the same symptoms as for major depression, except for suicidality, but requires only three symptoms in all, so long as they have persisted over two years.

electroconvulsive therapy (ECT)	A treatment for severe depression that involves passing a low-voltage electric current through the brain. The person is under anesthesia at the time of treatment. ECT is not commonly used in children and adolescents.
electroencephalography (EEG)	A method of recording the electrical activity in the brain through electrodes attached to the scalp.
episode	A specific period of mania or depression.
functional magnetic resonance imaging (fMRI)	Brain imaging technique based on changes in blood flow and oxygenation in the brain.
hallucination	"Phantom" sensations (sight, sound, touch, taste, and smell) that appear to be real even though they do not exist.
hippocampus	A seahorse-shaped structure located within the brain and considered an important part of the limbic system. It functions in learning, memory, and emotion.
hypomania	A mild form of mania, characterized by a persistently elevated, expansive, or irritable mood.
limbic system	A group of brain structures—including the amygdala, hippocampus, septum, and basal ganglia—that work to help regulate emotion, memory, and certain aspects of movement.
lithium	Oldest and best-known mood-stabilizing drug. Used in the treatment of bipolar disorder.
major depressive disorder	Major depression, also known as clinical depression or unipolar depression, is a type of depressive disorder characterized by a long-lasting depressed mood or marked loss of interest or pleasure in nearly all activities. The *DSM-IV* lists nine symptoms of major depression, five or more of which must be present over the same two-week period, including one of the first two: feeling depressed most of the day, nearly every day, or markedly diminished pleasure. There are several different subtypes of major depression.

mania	Feelings of intense mental and physical hyperactivity, elevated mood, and agitation.
manic depression	See bipolar disorder.
melancholic depression	A subtype of major depression with an emphasis on lack of pleasure or lack of reactivity to pleasure. Other characteristics include (three or more): depressed mood, depression at worst in the morning, early morning awakening, psychomotor agitation or retardation, significant weight loss, and inappropriate guilt.
mixed episodes	One of the mood episodes that compose bipolar disorder. A state that rapidly fluctuates between major depressive episodes and mania.
monoamine neurotransmitters	A group of neurotransmitters derived from certain kinds of amino acids. Monoamine neurotransmitters include dopamine, norepinephrine, and serotonin.
monoamine oxidase inhibitors (MAOIs)	A type of antidepressant that works by blocking monoamine oxidase, an enzyme that degrades monoamine neurotransmitters.
mood	A relatively long-lasting affective or emotional state.
mood disorder	An abnormal mental condition that affects a person's conscious state of mind and emotions. Mood disorders include bipolar disorder and depression.
mood stabilizers	Drugs, such as lithium and valproic acid, that are effective at treating mania, mood cycling, and shifting but are not effective at treating depression.
neurons (nerve cells)	Specialized cells that carry "messages" through an electrochemical process that uses electrical signals and chemical substances called neurotransmitters.
neurotransmitters	Chemical substances that transmit information between neurons. Neurotransmitters are released by neurons into the extracellular space at synapses. There are several different neurotransmitters, including acetylcholine, dopamine, gamma aminobutyric acid (GABA), norepinephrine, and serotonin.

norepinephrine	Also called noradrenaline. It is a monoamine neurotransmitter, produced both in the brain and in the peripheral nervous system. It seems to be involved in arousal, reward, regulation of sleep and mood, and the regulation of blood pressure.
obsessive-compulsive disorder (OCD)	A chronic anxiety disorder most commonly characterized by obsessive, distressing, intrusive thoughts and related compulsions.
positron emission tomography (PET)	Nuclear medicine imaging technique that measures gamma rays and reveals the functional process of the brain or other organs.
placebo (sugar pill)	A technique or medication that contains no active ingredient and therefore presumably has no physical benefit. Placebos are generally administered in such a way that the recipients believe they are receiving the active treatment.
psychiatrist	A medical doctor (MD) who specializes in treating mental diseases. A psychiatrist evaluates a person's mental health along with his or her physical health and can prescribe medications.
psychoanalysis	A therapeutic method, originated by Sigmund Freud, for treating mental disorders by investigating the interaction of conscious and unconscious elements in the patient's mind and bringing repressed fears and conflicts into the conscious mind, using techniques such as dream interpretation and free association.
psychologist	A mental health professional who has received specialized training in the study of the mind and emotions. A psychologist usually has an advanced degree, such as a PhD.
psychotherapy	A treatment method for mental illness in which a patient discusses his or her problems and feelings with a psychiatrist, psychologist, or counselor. Psychotherapy can help individuals change their thought or behavior patterns or understand how past experiences affect current behaviors.
psychotic depression	A rare subtype of major depression characterized by delusions or hallucinations, such as believing you are someone you are not, and hearing voices.

rapid cycling	Bipolar disorder cycling in which the patient abruptly alternates between episodes of depression and mania.
selective serotonin reuptake inhibitors (SSRIs)	A group of antidepressants that work by preventing the reuptake of the neurotransmitter serotonin, thus maintaining higher levels of serotonin in the brain.
serotonin	A monoamine neurotransmitter that regulates many functions, including mood, appetite, and sensory perception.
synapse	The site where neurons communicate with each other.
tricyclics	The oldest group of antidepressants. Tricyclics work by blocking the reuptake of several different neurotransmitters, including serotonin and norepinephrine.
unipolar depression	Another term for major depression. People who have unipolar depression do not cycle between depressive and elevated mood states.
valproic acid	A mood-stabilizing drug used for the treatment of bipolar disorder, convulsions, and migraines. Depakote is a brand name for valproic acid.

CHRONOLOGY

ca. 460 B.C.–A.D. 200 The ancient Greek theory of the four humors, ascribed by Hippocrates (460–370 B.C.) and extended by Galen (A.D. 131–200) held that the health of the body was represented by blood, phlegm, choler, and black bile. Traits that describe depression were associated with black bile, while those that describe mania were associated with choler.

A.D. 150 First written account of bipolar disorder in adolescence is described by Aretaeus of Cappadocia: "In those periods of life with which much heat and blood are associated, persons are most given to mania, namely, those about puberty, young men, and such as possess general vigor."

ca. 900 Muslim psychologist Ishaq ibn Imran's essay entitled *Maqala fi-l-Malikhuliya* refers to a mood disorder known as "malikhuliya," translated as "melancholia." The book *Leechdom, Wortcunning and Star Craft of Early England* gives herbal remedies for melancholia, as well as hallucinations, mental vacancy, dementia, and folly.

ca. 1020 Persian physician Avicenna's *The Canon of Medicine* describes a number of neuropsychiatric conditions, including melancholia and mania.

1621 Robert Burton publishes *The Anatomy of Melancholy*.

1695 Humphrey Ridley publishes *The Anatomy of the Brain.*

1755 J.B. Le Roy uses electroconvulsive therapy for mental illness.

1812 Benjamin Rush writes the first American book on psychiatry, *Medical Inquiries and Observations upon the Diseases of the Mind.*

1817 Lithium is discovered.

1849 British psychiatrist John Charles Bucknill uses electrical stimulation of the skin and potassium oxide to treat asylum patients with melancholic depression.

1854 French psychiatrist Jean-Pierre Falret describes a condition called "circular insanity" where a patient would switch from a state of manic excitement to a state of severe depression, while French neurologist Jules Baillarger describes "dual-form insanity."

1880 Seven categories of mental illness are used for U.S. census data: mania, melancholia, monomania, paresis, dementia, dipsomania, and epilepsy.

1881 German psychiatrist Emil Kraepelin writes *Compendium der Psychiatrie*, in which he first presents a classification of mental disorders. Kraepelin made an important differentiation between manic-depressive psychosis (bipolar disorder) and schizophrenia.

Late 1800s British physician Sir Alfred Garrod describes lithium as therapeutic for mood disorders caused by "gout retroceding to the head."

1903 British neurologist Thomas R. Elliott proposes the concept of chemical neurotransmitters.

1909 Clifford Beers founds the organization currently named Mental Health America.

1913 Kraepelin establishes the modern concept of manic-depressive illness as separate from schizophrenia ("dementia praecox") and includes the more common form of recurrent severe depression as well as the less common form of alternating periods of mania and depression.

1917 Sigmund Freud publishes *Mourning and Melancholia.*

1938 Ugo Cerletti and Lucino Bini treat human patients with electroshock therapy.

1949 Australian psychiatrist John Cade is the first to write a paper proposing the use of lithium to treat acute mania.

1951 The first modern antidepressant, called iproniazid, is discovered while doctors are studying tuberculosis medications. Iproniazid is a monoamine oxidase inhibitor (MAOI).

1952 The first edition of the *Diagnostic and Statistical Manual of Mental Disorders (DSM-I)* is published by the American Psychiatric Association.

1953 Betty Twarog and Irvine Page identify serotonin in the brain.

1956 Roland Kuhn discovers the antidepressant effects of imipramine, a tricyclic antidepressant.

1957 Arvid Carlsson demonstrates that dopamine is a brain neurotransmitter.

1960 Psychiatrist Thomas Szasz publishes *The Myth of Mental Illness,* in which he says there is no such thing as mental illness.

1969 Swedish psychiatrist Anna-Lise Linell reports success treating manic depression with lithium in children as young as six.

1960s A handful of articles in the medical literature observe that many adult bipolar patients have been ill since adolescence. Leading psychiatrists insist that to diagnose manic depression in children, they must meet adult criteria. Young patients are routinely diagnosed as schizophrenic "until proven otherwise."

1970 Lithium is approved by the Food and Drug Administration (FDA) to treat mania.

1973 Anticonvulsants are first used in treatment of bipolar disorder.

1975 The National Institute of Mental Health Conference on Depression in Childhood officially recognizes depression in children.

1970s Researchers at Eli Lilly, including Ray Fuller, Bryan Molloy, and David Wong, begin studying selective serotonin reuptake inhibitors (SSRIs). Their work leads to the discovery of Prozac.

1980 The American Psychiatric Association publishes the *DSM-III,* and bipolar disorder replaces manic-depressive disorder as a diagnostic term.

1987   Prozac is approved for use by the FDA.

1994   The American Psychiatric Association publishes the *DSM-IV*, which includes childhood mood disorders.

1995   Depakote (valproic acid) is approved by the FDA to treat bipolar disorder.

2001   Eli Lilly's patent on Prozac expires.

2004   The FDA orders pharmaceutical companies to put "black box" warnings on the labels of antidepressants to advise consumers that the medications could cause suicidal tendencies in individuals younger than age eighteen.

2006   The FDA extends the black-box warnings to young adults aged eighteen to twenty-four years.

ORGANIZATIONS TO CONTACT

The editors have compiled the following list of organizations concerned with the issues debated in this book. The descriptions are derived from materials provided by the organizations. All have publications or information available for interested readers. The list was compiled on the date of publication of the present volume; the information provided here may change. Be aware that many organizations take several weeks or longer to respond to inquiries, so allow as much time as possible.

Alliance for Human Research Protection
142 West End Ave.
Ste. 28P
New York, NY 10023
www.ahrp.org

AHRP is a national network of lay people and professionals dedicated to advancing responsible and ethical medical research practices and exposing corruption in the field of health care. The group speaks out against the widespread prescribing of antidepressants and other drugs. They publish online news articles about medical fraud and corruption.

American Foundation for Suicide Prevention (AFSP)
120 Wall St.
22nd Fl.
New York, NY 10005
(888) 333-2377
fax: (212) 363-6237
www.afsp.org

AFSP is a nonprofit organization dedicated to reducing loss of life from suicide. The AFSP works to prevent suicides and reach out and assist those who have been affected by suicide. The organization sponsors local "Out of the Darkness Overnight Walks" to bring people together who have been touched by suicide and to bring awareness to suicide prevention. AFSP's quarterly newsletter *Lifesavers* helps the AFSP to communicate and disseminate information about depression and suicide prevention to the public.

American Psychiatric Association (APA)
1000 Wilson Blvd.
Ste. 1825
Arlington, VA 22209-3901
(888) 357-7924
www.psych.org

The APA is an organization of professionals working in the field of psychiatry. The APA works to advance the profession and promote the highest quality care for individuals with mental illnesses and their families. Additionally, the APA educates the public about mental health, psychiatry, and successful treatment options. The organization publishes the twice-monthly newsletter *Psychiatric News,* as well as several journals, including the *American Journal of Psychiatry* and *Psychiatric Services.*

Child and Adolescent Bipolar Foundation (CABF)
1000 Skokie Blvd.
Ste. 570
Wilmette, IL 60091
(847) 256-8525
fax: (847) 920-9498
www.bpkids.org

CABF is a parent-led, nonprofit organization that seeks to raise public awareness about bipolar disorder and to improve the lives of families raising children and teens living with bipolar disorder and related conditions. The organization advocates for families and provides educational information about bipolar disorder. The organization's printed materials include the *Pediatric Bipolar Disorder Fact Sheet*, a flyer about the Child and Adolescent Bipolar Foundation for distribution to families, and a brochure for educators titled *Educating the Child with Bipolar Disorder.*

Dana Foundation: Dana Alliance for Brain Initiatives (DABI)
745 Fifth Ave.
Ste. 900
New York, NY 10151
(212) 223-4040
fax: (212) 593-7623
www.dana.org

The Dana Foundation is a private philanthropic organization with principal interests in brain science, immunology, and arts education. DABI is a nonprofit organization of neuroscientists committed to advancing public awareness about the progress and promise of brain research and to disseminating information on the brain in an understandable and accessible fashion. DABI organizes and coordinates the international Brain Awareness Week campaign and presents the *Gray Matters* radio series on Public Radio International. Dana Foundation publications include *Cerebrum*, an online journal of opinion with articles and book reviews exploring the impact of brain research on daily life and society and *BrainWork*, providing the latest in neuroscience research six times a year.

Depression and Bipolar Support Alliance (DBSA)
730 N. Franklin St.
Ste. 501
Chicago, Illinois
60610-7224
(800) 826 -3632
fax: (312) 642-7243
www.dbsalliance.org

DBSA is a leading patient-directed national organization focusing on depression and bipolar disease, the two most prevalent mental illnesses. The organization provides up-to-date information about mental illness, holds an annual depression and bipolar conference, supports mental health research, and sponsors hundreds of grassroots support groups across the country. DBSA publishes more than two dozen educational materials about living with mood disorders.

International Foundation for Research and Education on Depression (iFred)
2017-D Renard Ct.
Annapolis, MD 21401
(410) 268-0044
fax: (443) 782-0739
www.ifred.org

The iFred is a nonprofit organization dedicated to researching the causes of depression, supporting those dealing with depression, and combating the stigma associated with depression. iFred publishes a brochure and the *Startling Statistics* publication.

International Society for Bipolar Disorders (ISBD)
PO Box 7168
Pittsburgh, PA 15213-0168
(412) 802-6940
fax: (412) 802-6941
www.isbd.org

The ISBD is a global network of individuals dedicated to finding ways to improve the lives of those with bipolar disorder through collaboration, research, and education. *Bipolar Disorders: An International Journal of Psychiatry and Neurosciences* is the official journal of the society.

Mental Health America
2000 N. Beauregard St.
6th Fl.
Alexandria, VA 22311
(703) 684-7722
fax: (703) 684-5968
www.mentalhealth
america.net

Mental Health America (formerly known as the National Mental Health Association) is a nonprofit organization dedicated to helping all people live mentally healthier lives. The organization educates the public about ways to preserve and strengthen its mental health; fights for access to effective mental health care; fights to end discrimination against people with mental and addictive disorders; and fosters innovative mental health research, treatment, and support services. Mental Health America issues several e-mail newsletters, such as *The Bell*, and produces several fact sheets and informational documents.

National Alliance on Mental Illness (NAMI)
2107 Wilson Blvd.
Ste. 300
Arlington, VA 22201-3042
(703) 524-7600
fax: (703) 524-9094
www.nami.org

NAMI is a national grassroots mental health organization that seeks to eradicate mental illness and improve the lives of persons living with serious mental illness and their families. NAMI works through advocacy, research, education, and support. The organization publishes a periodic magazine called the *Advocate*.

National Institute of Mental Health (NIMH)
Science Writing, Press, and Dissemination Branch
6001 Executive Blvd.
Rm. 8184, MSC 9663
Bethesda, MD 20892-9663
(866) 615-6464
fax: (301) 443-4279
www.nimh.nih.gov

The NIMH is the leading agency of the U.S. government concerned with mental health issues. The agency's mission is to reduce the burden of mental illness and behavioral disorders through research on mind, brain, and behavior. The NIMH publishes various booklets, fact sheets, and easy-to-read materials on mental health issues.

**Society for
Neuroscience (SFN)**
1121 Fourteenth St. NW
Ste. 1010
Washington, DC 20005
(202) 962-4000
fax: (202) 962-4941
www.sfn.org

The SFN works to provide professional development activities and educational resources for neuroscientists and to educate the public about the findings, applications, and potential of neuroscience research. The organization has several online publications, including *Brain Backgrounders*, an online series of articles that answer basic neuroscience questions, and *Brain Briefings*, a monthly two-page newsletter explaining how basic neuroscience discoveries lead to clinical applications.

FOR FURTHER READING

Books

Richard Berlin, ed., *Poets on Prozac*. Baltimore: Johns Hopkins University Press, 2008.

Norman Doidge, *The Brain That Changes Itself: Stories of Personal Triumph from the Frontiers of Brain Science*. New York: Penguin, 2007.

Ronald W. Dworkin, *Artificial Unhappiness: The Dark Side of the New Happy Class*. New York: Carroll & Graf, 2006.

Frederick Goodwin and Kay Jamison, *Manic-Depressive Illness: Bipolar Disorders and Recurrent Depression*. New York: Oxford University Press, 2007.

Marya Hornbacher, *Madness: A Bipolar Life*. Boston: Houghton Mifflin, 2008.

Allan V. Horwitz and Jerome C. Wakefield, *The Loss of Sadness: How Psychiatry Transformed Normal Sorrow into Depressive Disorder*. New York: Oxford University Press USA, 2007.

Paul Keedwell, *How Sadness Survived: The Evolutionary Basis of Depression*. Abingdon, UK: Radcliffe, 2008.

Darian Leader, *The New Black: Mourning, Melancholia and Depression*. New York: Penguin, 2008.

Gwyneth Lewis, *Sunbathing in the Rain*. Philadelphia: Jessica Kingsley, 2007.

Emily Martin, *Bipolar Expeditions: Mania and Depression in American Culture*. Princeton, NJ: Princeton University Press, 2007.

Jeffrey Schwartz and Sharon Begley, *The Mind and the Brain: Neuroplasticity and the Power of Mental Force*. New York: HarperPerennial, 2003.

Kate Scowen, *My Kind of Sad: What It's Like to Be Young and Depressed*. New York: Annick, 2006.

Edward Shorter, *Losing Ground: The Troubled History of Mood Disorders in Psychiatry*. New York: Oxford University Press, 2008.

Periodicals

Stephanie Armour, "Workplaces Quit Quietly Ignoring Mental Illness," *USA Today*, August 22, 2006.

David Armstrong and Keith J. Winstein, "Antidepressants Scrutinized over Efficacy," *Washington Post*, January 17, 2008. http://online.wsj.com/article/SB120051950205895415.html.

Charles Barber, "The Medicated Americans: Antidepressant Prescriptions on the Rise," *Scientific American*, February 2008.

Sharon Begley, "Happiness: Enough Already," *Newsweek*, February 2, 2008.

Benedict Carey, "Hypomanic? Absolutely. But Oh So Productive!" *New York Times*, March 22, 2005. www.nytimes.com/2005/03/22/health/psychology/22hypo.html?_r=1&oref=slogin.

J. Raymond DePaulo Jr., "Bipolar Disorder Treatment: An Evidence-Based Reality Check," *American Journal of Psychiatry*, February 2006. http://ajp.psychiatryonline.org/cgi/content/full/163/2/175.

Richard A. Friedman, "Who Are We? Coming of Age on Antidepressants," *New York Times*, April 15, 2008. www.nytimes.com/2008/04/l5/health/l5mind.html?_r=3&adxnnl=l&oref=slogin&adxnnlx=1214064292-KReJQKlecd6IT9Gu+NGEBg.

S. Nassir Ghaemi, "Hippocrates and Prozac: The Controversy About Antidepressants in Bipolar Disorder," *Primary Psychiatry*, 2006. www.primarypsychiatry.com/aspx/ArticleDetail.aspx?articleid=751.

Ben Goldacre, "A Quick Fix Would Stop Drug Firms Bending the Truth," *Guardian*, February 27, 2008. www.badscience.net/?p=619.

Peter D. Kramer, "Sunny-Side Up," *Slate*, January 22, 2008. www.slate.com/id/2182585/pagenum/all/.

Elizabeth Landau, "Experts Ponder Link Between Creativity, Mood Disorders," *CNN.com*, October 7, 2008. www.cnn.com/2008/HEALTH/conditions/10/07/creativity.depression/.

Anne McIlroy, "Meditating Through Mental Illness," *Toronto Globe & Mail*, August 15, 2008.

Tami Port, "Personality Versus Mood Disorder: How These Categories of Mental Illness Differ," *Suite101.com*, August 12, 2007. http://personalitydisorders.suite101.com/article.cfm/personality_versus_mood_disorder.

Kimberly Read and Marcia Purse, "Mood Disorders and Sleep," About.com, June 20, 2006. http://bipolar.about.com/cs/sleep/a/0002_mood_sleep.htm.

Tina Hesman Saey, "Growing Up to Prozac: Drug Makes New Neurons Mature Faster," *Science News*, February 9, 2008.

INDEX